Spelling
Linking Words to Meaning
LEVEL 3

John R. Pescosolido
Professor Emeritus
Central Connecticut State University
New Britain, Connecticut

Reviewers

Maria Driend
Literacy Coordinator
Cooperative Education Services
Trumbull, Connecticut

Terese D'Amico
Gifted Education Specialist for Grades 3–6
Thomas Jefferson Magnet School
Euclid City Schools
Euclid, Ohio

Patricia D'Amore
Assistant Reading Coordinator
Cooperative Educational Services
Trumbull, Connecticut

Dr. Donna Ronzone
Principal and Director of Special Education
Briggs Elementary School District
Santa Paula, California

STECK-VAUGHN
ELEMENTARY · SECONDARY · ADULT · LIBRARY

A Harcourt Company

www.steck-vaughn.com

Acknowledgments

Editorial Director Stephanie Muller
Senior Editor Amanda Sperry
Assistant Editor Julie M. Smith
Associate Director of Design Cynthia Ellis
Senior Design Manager Cynthia Hannon
Designer Deborah Diver
Media Researcher Sarah Fraser
Editorial Development, Design, and Production The Quarasan Group, Inc.
Cover Illustration Dale Verzaal
Senior Technical Advisor Alan Klemp

PHOTO CREDITS

3 ©James Darell/Stone; 5 ©Ron Austing/Frank Lane Picture Agency/Corbis; 6 ©Mary Kate Denny/Stone; 8 ©Jeff Smith/FOTOSMITH; 10 top (t) ©James Darell/Stone; bottom (b) ©David Young-Wolff/PhotoEdit, Inc.; 11 (juice and water) ©PhotoDisc, Inc; (fruit) ©Comstock, Inc.; (child) ©Ruth Anderson, Bruce Esbin/Photo Network/PictureQuest; 12 ©PhotoDisc, Inc.; 13 ©PhotoDisc, Inc.; 14 ©Myrleen Ferguson/PhotoEdit, Inc.; 15 ©David Young-Wolff/PhotoEdit, Inc.; 16 ©PhotoDisc, Inc.; 17 ©Lori Adamski Peek/Stone; 18 (t) ©Lori Adamski Peek/Stone; (b) ©Roy Morsch/The Stock Market; 20 ©Corbis; 21 ©PhotoDisc, Inc.; 26 ©PhotoDisc, Inc.; 30 ©PhotoDisc, Inc.; 32 ©Mark E. Gibson/DRK Photo; 36 ©Bojan Brecelj/Corbis; 34 (t) ©Mark Richards/PhotoEdit, Inc.; (b) ©Michael Newman/PhotoEdit, Inc.; 34-35 ©PhotoDisc, Inc.; 35 ©CAROLCO/TRI-STAR/The Kobal Collection; 39 left (l) ©PhotoDisc, Inc.; right (r) ©C Squared Studios/PhotoDisc, Inc.; 41 ©Lori Adamski Peek/Stone ; 42 ©Corbis; 47 ©Corbis; 48 ©Mary Kate Denny/PhotoEdit, Inc.; 53 ©Quarto, Inc./Artville; 54 ©David Hanover/Stone; 56 (portrait) ©Myles Pinkney; (cup of brushes) ©PhotoDisc, Inc.; (brush) ©Joe Atlas/Artville; (pencils) ©Artville; 57 Sam and the Tigers published by Penguin Putnam, Home Place published by Simon & Schuster; 58 ©Myles Pinkney; 59 ©John Michael/International Stock; 60 ©Myrleen Ferguson/PhotoEdit, Inc.; 66 ©Bob Daemmrich/Stock Boston/PictureQuest; 72 ©Corbis; 73 ©PhotoDisc, Inc.; 75 ©Tim McGuire, Jim Cummins Studio/FPG International; 76 ©Comstock, Inc.; 82 ©Corbis; 84 (t) ©Hulton-Deutsch Collection/Corbis; (b) ©Museum of History & Industry/Corbis; 85 ©Ewing Galloway/Index Stock Imagery/PictureQuest; 86 ©Hulton-Deutsch Collection/Corbis; 88 ©Planet Earth Pictures/FPG International; 90 (t) ©SuperStock, Inc.; (b) ©Planet Earth Pictures/FPG International; 91 ©J. Sneesby & B. Wilkins/Stone; 92 (t) ©SuperStock, Inc.; (b) ©PhotoDisc, Inc.; 94 ©Otto Rogge/The Stock Market; 98 ©Corbis; 100 ©Telegraph Colour Library/FPG International; 106 ©PhotoDisc, Inc.; 107 ©SuperStock, Inc.; 108 ©Digital Studios; 109 ©Walter Bibikow/FPG International; 110 ©PhotoDisc, Inc.; 115 ©Corel Corporation; 116 ©Corbis; 122 ©Victoria Pearson/Stone; 126 ©Corel Corporation; 128 ©PhotoDisc, Inc.; 133 ©Digital Studios; 134 ©Comstock, Inc.; 136 (t) ©G.K. & Vikki Hart/PhotoDisc, Inc.; (b) ©Ryan McVay/PhotoDisc, Inc.; 137 ©Kathi Lamm/Stone; 138 ©G.K. & Vikki Hart/PhotoDisc, Inc.; 139 ©RubberBall Productions; 140 ©Image provided by MetaTools; 141 (l) ©Digital Studios; (r) ©PhotoDisc, Inc.; 143 ©Corbis; 144 ©Peter Cade/Stone; 145 ©PhotoDisc, Inc.; 148 ©PhotoDisc, Inc.; 149 ©PhotoDisc, Inc.; 150 ©Renee Lynn/Stone; 154 ©Roger Tidman/Corbis; 156 ©Digital Vision Photography/Eyewire, Inc.; 158 ©Bettmann/Corbis; 159 ©Hulton-Deutsch Collection/Corbis; 160 ©Bettmann/Corbis; 162 ©David Young-Wolff/PhotoEdit, Inc.; 168 ©Sonda Dawes/The Image Works; 173 ©Don Spiro/Stone; 174 ©PhotoDisc, Inc.; 175 ©Geostock/PhotoDisc, Inc.; 177 ©David Young-Wolff/PhotoEdit, Inc.; 178 ©PhotoDisc, Inc.; 184 ©Corbis; 185 ©PhotoDisc, Inc.; 186 (t) ©Paul Harris/Stone; middle (m) ©PhotoDisc, Inc.; (b) ©Felicia Martinez/PhotoEdit, Inc.; 187 (t) ©PhotoDisc, Inc.; (b) ©Lori Adamski Peek/Stone; 188 ©Paul Harris/Stone; 190 ©Corbis; 192 (t) ©Ron Austing/Frank Lane Picture Agency/Corbis; (bl) ©Joe McDonald/Corbis; (br) ©Wolfgang Kaehler/Corbis; 193 (l) ©W. Perry Conway/Corbis; (r) ©Kennan Ward/Corbis; 194 ©Wolfgang Kaehler/Corbis; 196 ©FPG International; 197 ©Quarto, Inc./Artville; 200 ©David Young-Wolff/PhotoEdit, Inc.; 202 ©PhotoDisc, Inc.; 206 ©PhotoDisc, Inc.; 208 (t) ©PhotoDisc, Inc.; (b) ©PhotoDisc, Inc.; 209 (l) ©Comstock, Inc.; (r) ©Image Farm; 211 ©PhotoDisc, Inc.; 219 ©Corbis; 224 ©Corbis; 225 ©Corbis; 229 ©iSwoop; 236 ©PhotoDisc, Inc.; 240 ©PhotoDisc, Inc. All Dictionary photos by Corbis, iSwoop, PhotoDisc, Steck-Vaughn Collection.

ART CREDITS

Bernard Adnet 155; Marilynn Barr 68–70, 204–206; Lynda Calvert–Weyant 123; Randy Chewning 152–154, 174, 191; David Austin Clar 151, 157, 175 (t); Mark Corcoran 28–30; Doug Cushman 163, 189; Karen Dugan 78–80, 129, 198–200; Cecile Duray–Bito 22–23; Allan Eitzen 44–46; Doris Ettlinger 55, 195; Peter Fasolino 38, 89; Cynthia Fisher 73 (t); Ruth Flanigan 27, 43, 101, 118–120, 170–172, 183; Susan Guevara 49, 99, 106; Laurie Hamilton 62–64, 107, 146–148; Laura Jacobsen 33, 83, 180–182; John Kanzler 72; Cheryl Kirk-Noll 50–52; John Lund 61, 164–166; Erin Mauterer 39, 96–98, 112–114, 169, 203; Michael Morris 140; Kathleen O'Malley 37, 102–104; Cary Pillo 9; Daniel Powers 77, 179; Stacey Schuett 111; Jeff Shelly 67, 117; Krystyna Stasiak 40, 73 (b); B.K. Taylor 95, 124–126; Jackie Urbanovic 135; Jason Wolff 130–132, 175 (b).

Pronunciation key and diacritical marks copyright © 1998 by Houghton Mifflin Company. Adapted and reproduced by permission from *The American Heritage Student Dictionary*.

Steck-Vaughn Spelling: Linking Words to Meaning is a registered trademark of Steck-Vaughn Company.

Softcover ISBN 0-7398-3611-0   Hardcover ISBN 0-7398-5055-5

The words *soil, worm, eggs, flower,* and *bird* are hidden on the cover. Can you find them?

Contents

Unit 1

Unit 2

Unit 3

Unit 4

Unit 5

Unit 6

Study Steps to Learn a Word

 Say the word. What consonant sounds do you hear? What vowel sounds do you hear? How many syllables do you hear?

 Look at the letters in the word. Think about how each sound is spelled. Find any spelling patterns or parts that you know. Close your eyes. Picture the word in your mind.

 Spell the word aloud.

 Write the word. Say each letter as you write it.

⑤ Check the spelling. If you did not spell the word correctly, use the study steps again.

Use the steps on this page to study words that are hard for you.

6

Spelling Strategies

What can you do when you aren't sure how to spell a word?

Say the word aloud. Make sure you say it correctly. Listen to the sounds in the word. Think about letters and patterns that might spell the sounds.

Look in the Spelling Table to find common spellings for sounds in the word.

Think about related words. They may help you spell the word you're not sure of.

child—children

Guess the spelling of the word and check it in a dictionary.

Write the word in different ways. Compare the spellings and choose the one that looks correct.

trane   tran   (train)   trayn

Think about any spelling rules you know that can help you spell the word.

Most plural words are formed by adding -s.

Choose a rhyming helper and use it. A rhyming helper is a word that rhymes with the word and is spelled like it.

strong—song

Break the word into syllables and think about how each syllable might be spelled.

No vem ber
for got

Create a memory clue, such as a rhyme.

Write i before e, except after c.

Words with Short *a*

catch

1. *a* Words

_____
_____
_____
_____
_____
_____
_____
_____
_____
_____
_____
_____
_____
_____
_____

2. *au* Word

_____

ask
matter
black
add
match
Saturday
class
apple
subtract
laugh
thank
catch
January
after
hammer
half

Say and Listen

Say each spelling word. Listen for the short *a* sound.

Think and Sort

Look at the letters in each word. Think about how short *a* is spelled. Spell each word aloud.

Short *a* can be shown as /ă/. How many spelling patterns for /ă/ do you see?

1. Write the spelling words that have the *a* pattern.

2. Write the spelling word that has the *au* pattern.

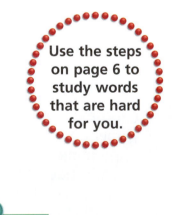

Use the steps on page 6 to study words that are hard for you.

Spelling Patterns

a	au
m**a**tch	l**au**gh

Spelling and Meaning

Definitions   Write the spelling word for each definition.
Use the Spelling Dictionary if you need to.

1. to find the sum   _____
2. problem   _____
3. to look alike   _____
4. group of students   _____
5. following   _____
6. to say one is grateful   _____
7. one of two equal parts   _____
8. to request   _____

Classifying   Write the spelling word that belongs in each group.

9. banana   orange   pear   _____
10. add   multiply   divide   _____
11. screwdriver saw   drill   _____
12. white   green   yellow   _____
13. chuckle   grin   smile   _____
14. March   April   September   _____
15. run   throw   pitch   _____

Word Story   One of the spelling words comes from two Old English words. The first is *Saeter*. The second is *daeg*. *Saeter* was the name for the Roman god Saturn. *Daeg* meant "day." Write the word.

16. _____

Family Tree: *thank*   Think about how the *thank* words are alike in spelling and meaning. Then add another *thank* word to the tree.

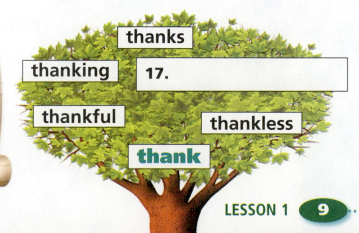

thanks

thanking

17.

thankful

thankless

thank

Use each spelling word once to complete the selection.

Cold Relief

Your head feels as if it is being pounded with a _____.
1
Your eyes are so itchy and watery that you can't see well. You put on socks that do not _____. Your throat
2
hurts. You sniffle and sneeze your way through every _____ at
3
school. What is the _____?
4
You have a cold!

You may think that you _____ colds from cold,
5
wet weather. This is not true. Icy winds in _____ or
6
February do not cause colds. You can _____ tiny
7
germs called cold viruses for your sniffles and sneezes.

Cold germs travel in the air and on people's hands, so you should wash your hands often. Washing your hands is especially important _____
8
being around someone else who has a cold. You can also _____
9
people who sneeze to cover their mouth.

Unfortunately, there is no cure for the common cold. There are some things you can do, however, that will make you feel better.

Drink lots of fruit juice and water. Drink at least ＿＿＿＿＿＿＿＿ a glass every

_10_

hour. A full glass is even better.

People say that an ＿＿＿＿＿＿＿＿

_11_

a day keeps the doctor away. It is true that apples and other good foods help make your body strong. When you have a cold, ＿＿＿＿＿＿＿＿

_12_

extra fruits and vegetables to your meals. At the same time,

＿＿＿＿＿＿＿＿ potato chips,

_13_

candy, and other junk foods.

Some people think that chicken soup is the best medicine for a cold. Do not ＿＿＿＿＿＿＿＿. Hot

_14_

soup really can make you feel better. Some people say that adding a little bit of ＿＿＿＿＿＿＿＿ pepper

_15_

makes the soup work even better.

When you have a cold, stay in bed and rest. This is true even if it is a sunny ＿＿＿＿＿＿＿＿

_16_

morning. If you take good care of yourself, you should feel better in no time!

ask
matter
black
add
match
Saturday
class
apple
subtract
laugh
thank
catch
January
after
hammer
half

Spelling and Writing

ask
matter
black
add
match
Saturday
class
apple
subtract
laugh
thank
catch
January
after
hammer
half

Write to the Point

Many people feel terrible when they have a cold. Have you ever had a cold? Write a paragraph about how you felt. Tell what you did to feel better. Try to use spelling words from this lesson in your paragraph.

Use the strategies on page 7 when you are not sure how to spell a word.

Proofreading

Proofread the ad for *Feelfine* apple juice below. Use proofreading marks to correct five spelling mistakes, three capitalization mistakes, and two punctuation mistakes.

Proofreading Marks

◯ spell correctly
≡ capitalize
⊙ add period

It's Janary You have the sniffles. did you cach a cold? to feel better fast, drink Feelfine.

It is the finest fruit juice ever made.

Look for the aple on the bottle. you will feel great affter only haf a glass

Dictionary Skills

Alphabetical Order   When words are in alphabetical order, they are in **ABC** order.

This group of words is in alphabetical order.

> **bend   friend   horse**

This group of words is <u>not</u> in alphabetical order.

> **egg   animal   chicken**

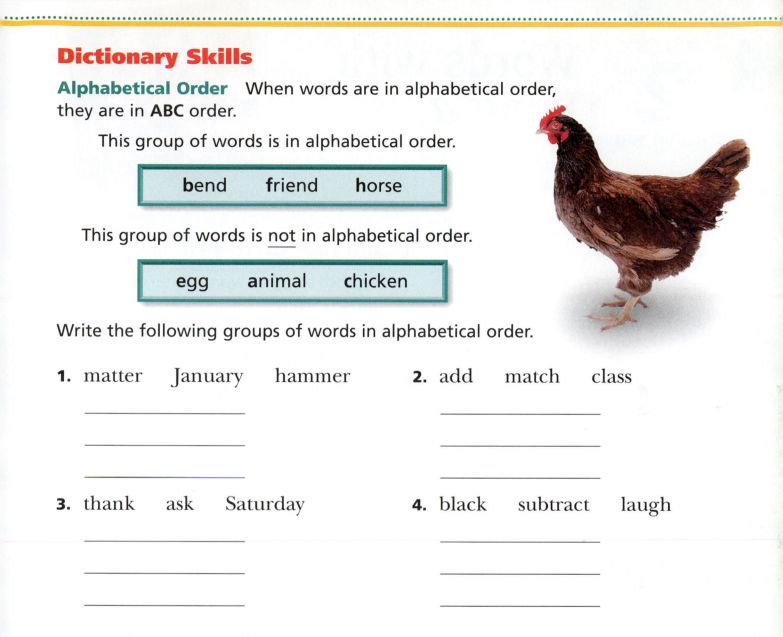

Write the following groups of words in alphabetical order.

1. matter   January   hammer

_____

_____

_____

2. add   match   class

_____

_____

_____

3. thank   ask   Saturday

_____

_____

_____

4. black   subtract   laugh

_____

_____

_____

Challenge Yourself

Use the Spelling Dictionary to answer these questions. Then use separate paper to write sentences showing that you understand the meaning of each Challenge Word.

Challenge Words

plaid	agony
clank	fragile

5. Does a **plaid** shirt have one color or many colors?   _____

6. Would you be in **agony** if you hit your thumb with a hammer?

_____

7. Could an old iron gate **clank** when you shut it?   _____

8. Would it be safe to play in a **fragile** tree house?   _____

Words with Long *a*

break

1. *a*-consonant-*e* Words

_____
_____
_____
_____
_____
_____
_____
_____
_____

2. *ay* Words

_____
_____
_____
_____

3. *ea* Words

_____
_____

4. *a* Word

_____

gray
page
great
change
April
face
save
away
break
ate
place
pay
late
safe
May
came

Say and Listen

Say each spelling word. Listen for the long *a* sound.

Think and Sort

Look at the letters in each word. Think about how long *a* is spelled. Spell each word aloud.

Long *a* can be shown as /ā/. How many spelling patterns for /ā/ do you see?

1. Write the **nine** spelling words that have the *a*-consonant-*e* pattern.

2. Write the **four** spelling words that have the *ay* pattern.

3. Write the **two** spelling words that have the *ea* pattern.

4. Write the **one** spelling word that has the *a* pattern.

Use the steps on page 6 to study words that are hard for you.

Spelling Patterns

a-consonant-e	ay	ea	a
face	May	break	April

Spelling and Meaning

Synonyms   Synonyms are words that have the same meaning. Write the spelling word that is a synonym for each word below.

1. arrived _____
2. unhurt _____
3. absent _____
4. put _____
5. messenger _____
6. wonderful _____
7. switch _____
8. silvery _____

Anagrams   An anagram is a word whose letters can be used to make another word. Write the spelling word that contains the letters of the underlined anagram in each sentence.

9. Jenna's birthday is in the month of <u>yaM</u>. _____

10. The team <u>tea</u> pizza after the game. _____

11. Please do not <u>brake</u> my pencil. _____

12. Ten dollars is too much to <u>yap</u>. _____

13. The bus was <u>tale</u> this morning. _____

14. Let's <u>vase</u> the best for last. _____

15. The baby had a big smile on her <u>cafe</u>. _____

Word Story   Many English words come from other languages. One spelling word comes from the Latin word *Aprilis*. *Aprilis* was the name of the second month in the Roman calendar. It names one of the spring months. Write the spelling word.

16. _____

Family Tree: *pay*   Think about how the *pay* words are alike in spelling and meaning. Then add another *pay* word to the tree.

pays

payer

17.

repay

payable

pay

Use each spelling word once to complete the selection.

A Special Day

Arbor Day is a special holiday. The word *arbor* means "tree." Arbor Day helps people remember to plant new trees and to

_____ older ones. It can help _____
1   2

people's ideas about Earth and the environment.

Arbor Day was started by a Nebraska man named Sterling Morton in 1872. Mr. Morton loved trees. He asked everyone in the state to plant trees on a day he called Arbor Day. He wanted to give prizes to those who planted the most trees. A million trees were planted. Imagine the look on Mr. Morton's _____! He
3
was very surprised and pleased. The day was a _____
4
success.

Soon people in other states started to celebrate Arbor Day, too. In 1876 a man in Connecticut wanted to honor the nation's hundredth birthday. The man invited children to plant trees. He said he would _____ one dollar to each child who planted
5
trees. He kept his promise.

Since that time children have always been part of Arbor Day celebrations. In 1882 almost 20,000 children in Cincinnati, Ohio, _____ from many schools to the city's Eden Park. They
6
planted new trees. They were careful not to _____ any
7
leaves or branches. Then the children named each tree after a famous

person. Perhaps they _____ 8 a picnic lunch.
They might even have read a _____ 9 from
a book about _____ 10 squirrels.

Over the years Arbor Day celebrations have taken
_____ 11 in city parks, public squares, and schools.
Today both children and adults take part in Arbor Day
events. Many people celebrate Arbor Day in March,
_____ 12, or _____ 13. Others celebrate
in _____ 14 fall or winter. Japan, China, and other
countries far _____ 15 celebrate this holiday, too.

Arbor Day is an important day. It is a day to think about
trees and ways to help keep them _____ 16. This
special day gives people a time to plant new life.

gray
page
great
change
April
face
save
away
break
ate
place
pay
late
safe
May
came

Spelling and Writing

gray
page
great
change
April
face
save
away
break
ate
place
pay
late
safe
May
came

Write to the Point

Posters help people learn about important events. Design a poster for Arbor Day. Use words that will make people want to help Earth by planting trees. Tell why trees are good for Earth and people. Try to use spelling words from this lesson in your poster.

Use the strategies on page 7 when you are not sure how to spell a word.

Proofreading

Proofread these directions for planting a tree. Use proofreading marks to correct five spelling mistakes, three capitalization mistakes, and two unnecessary words.

Proofreading Marks

⃝ spell correctly
≡ capitalize
ℰ take out

How to Plant a Tree

To plant a tree, first choose a saif spot. it should

be a playce far from houses and awey from from

strong winds. Plant the tree laete in the day when

the sun is low. dig a deep hole and save the soil.

then put the tree in the hole and

water it well. Be careful not to to

brek any branches on the tree. Last,

pack the soil around the tree.

Language Connection

Sentences Begin the first word of each sentence with a capital letter.

> **M**y sister collects postage stamps.

Put a period at the end of a sentence that tells something.

> The first postage stamp was made in England**.**

Use the spelling words in the boxes below to complete the story. Then use proofreading marks to correct mistakes in the use of capital letters and periods.

May   face   save   great   page   gray   away

heather likes to _____ stamps She must keep them _____ from Scooter, her _____ puppy. last _____ a _____ fell out of Heather's stamp book She looked all over for it. then she looked at Scooter The fur on his _____ was stuck together. he had a _____ time eating her stamps.

Challenge Yourself

What do you think each Challenge Word means? Check the Spelling Dictionary to see if you are right. Then use separate paper to write sentences showing that you understand the meaning of each Challenge Word.

Challenge Words	
cable	debate
dismay	labor

1. A **cable** holds up the bridge.

2. She will **debate** whether to buy a new bike or fix her old one.

3. I watched in **dismay** as my hat fell in the mud.

4. Riding up the steep hill required a great deal of **labor**.

More Words with Long *a*

train

1. *ai* Words

_____

_____

_____

_____

_____

_____

_____

_____

2. *a* Words

_____

_____

_____

_____

_____

3. *eigh* Words

_____

_____

4. *ey* Word

_____

fable

rain

danger

sail

afraid

table

aid

train

eight

wait

able

aim

weigh

they

paint

paper

Say and Listen

Say each spelling word. Listen for the long *a* sound.

Think and Sort

Look at the letters in each word. Think about how long *a* is spelled. Spell each word aloud.

Long *a* can be shown as /ā/. How many spelling patterns for /ā/ do you see?

1. Write the **eight** spelling words that have the *ai* pattern.

2. Write the **five** spelling words that have the *a* pattern.

3. Look at the word *eight*. The spelling pattern for this word is *eigh*. The *g* and *h* are silent. Write the **two** spelling words that have the *eigh* pattern.

4. Write the **one** spelling word that has the *ey* pattern.

Use the steps on page 6 to study words that are hard for you.

Spelling Patterns

ai	a	eigh	ey
r**ai**n	p**a**per	w**eigh**	th**ey**

Antonyms   Antonyms are words that have opposite meanings. Write the spelling word that is an antonym of each word below.

1. hurt _____
2. fearless _____
3. go _____
4. safety _____
5. unable _____

Analogies   An analogy shows that one pair of words is like another pair. Write the spelling word that completes each analogy.

6. *Bedspread* is to *bed* as *tablecloth* is to _____.
7. *Two* is to *four* as *four* is to _____.
8. *Car* is to *road* as _____ is to *track*.
9. *Engine* is to *car* as _____ is to *sailboat*.
10. *Story* is to _____ as *animal* is to *dog*.
11. *Silk* is to *smooth* as _____ is to *wet*.
12. *We* is to *us* as _____ is to *them*.
13. *Oven* is to *bake* as *scale* is to _____.
14. *Ink* is to *pen* as _____ is to *brush*.
15. *Easy* is to *simple* as _____ is to *point*.

Word Story   Long ago some people wrote on papyrus. Papyrus was made of dried grass. Today most people use another material to write on. It is made of finely cut wood. The name of this material comes from the word *papyrus*. Write the word.

16. _____

Family Tree: *paint*   Think about how the *paint* words are alike in spelling and meaning. Then add another *paint* word to the tree.

paints

painter | 17.

repaint | painted

paint

Use each spelling word once to complete the selection.

Make Your Own Village

What can you do when you can't go outside and play because of

_____? Make your own village! It's fun and easy to do.

1

First, spread pieces of paper on top of a _____.

2

Newspaper is a good kind of paper to use. Then,

cut more pieces of _____ into strips.

3

Mix one cup of flour with enough water to make a

thin paste. Gather seven or _____

4

small boxes to use for buildings.

Next, get a towel and wet it. Keep it near you as you work with

the paper and paste. The wet towel will _____ you in

5

cleaning your sticky hands.

Dip the strips of paper into the paste.

Don't be _____ to use a lot of

6

paste. Wind the paper strips around the

boxes. You will be _____ to

7

make buildings of different shapes by

using more strips in some places.

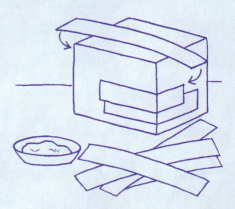

You should _____ to work until you have covered all

8

your buildings with paper strips. Then, let the buildings dry. You will

probably have to _____ a day or two for all the wet

9

paper to dry.

Later, get some _____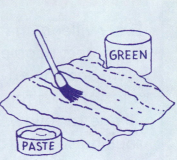
10

and brushes and paint your buildings. Then

you are ready to make the ground. Spread

the paste over wrinkled paper. Paint your

ground green after the paste dries. Then,

paint a lake. Make a boat to _____ on the lake.
11

Do you think your village needs a _____? You
12

can make one by using old matchboxes for the cars. Make

the train tracks out of toothpicks. For train wheels, buttons

work well because _____ are small and round.
13

You can also add mountains and bridges to your village.

You can even add a sign that says "Falling Rock" to warn

of _____.
14

What is missing from your village? People! Make clay

people. If they don't _____ too much, you can
15

sit them in your boat without making it turn over. You can

also use the people to act out a _____ or other
16

kind of story. Have fun playing with your village!

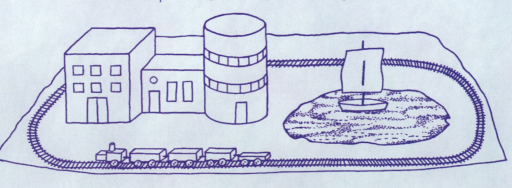

fable
rain
danger
sail
afraid
table
aid
train
eight
wait
able
aim
weigh
they
paint
paper

Spelling and Writing

fable
rain
danger
sail
afraid
table
aid
train
eight
wait
able
aim
weigh
they
paint
paper

Write to the Point

Every village and town has rules to protect people, the things they own, and the environment. Make a list of rules for the people of a village to follow. Try to use spelling words from this lesson.

Proofreading

Proofread the paragraph below. Use proofreading marks to correct five spelling mistakes, three capitalization mistakes, and two unnecessary words.

Please do not litter.

Use the strategies on page 7 when you are not sure how to spell a word.

Proofreading Marks

◯ spell correctly
≡ capitalize
ℓ take out

Mr. sanchez is the art teacher at our school. He teaches the third grade once a week. each class is abel to make many things. This week we are making things out of paper. our class has made a boat with with a large paper sail. Mrs. Digg's class has made a trane that that is aight feet long. Thay cannot wate to paint it.

Using the Spelling Table

Suppose that you need to find a word in a dictionary, but you're not sure how to spell one of the sounds. What can you do? You can use a spelling table to find the different ways that the sound can be spelled.

Let's say that you're not sure how to spell the last consonant sound in *sock*. Is it *k, c, ck,* or *ch*? First, find the pronunciation symbol for the sound in the Spelling Table on page 213. Then read the first spelling listed for /k/ and look up *sok* in the Spelling Dictionary. Look for each spelling in the dictionary until you find the correct one.

Sound	Spellings	Examples
/k/	k c ck ch	keep, coat, kick, school

Write the correct spelling for /k/ in each word below. Use the Spelling Table above and the Spelling Dictionary.

1. kable _____
2. karton _____
3. koarse _____
4. blak _____
5. blok _____
6. skeme _____
7. komb _____
8. subtrakt _____
9. klok _____
10. kard _____
11. korner _____
12. soks _____

Challenge Yourself

Use the Spelling Dictionary to answer these questions. Then use separate paper to write sentences showing that you understand the meaning of each Challenge Word.

Challenge Words

frail	agent
maintain	contain

13. Would a bridge made of toothpicks be **frail**? _____

14. Could a secret **agent** work for a government? _____

15. Is it important to **maintain** a town's bridges and roads?

_____

16. Are jars that **contain** jam empty? _____

egg

Lesson 4

Words with Short *e*

1. e Words
_____
_____
_____
_____
_____
_____
_____
_____
_____
_____

2. ea Words
_____
_____
_____

3. ai Words
_____
_____

4. ay Word
_____

next
egg
says
ready
end
help
spent
again
second
forget
dress
said
address
read
test
head

Say and Listen

Say each spelling word. Listen for the short e sound.

Think and Sort

Look at the letters in each word. Think about how short e is spelled. Spell each word aloud.

Short e can be shown as /ĕ/. How many spelling patterns for /ĕ/ do you see?

1. Write the **ten** spelling words that have the *e* pattern.

2. Write the **three** spelling words that have the *ea* pattern.

3. Write the **two** spelling words that have the *ai* pattern.

4. Write the **one** spelling word that has the *ay* pattern.

Use the steps on page 6 to study words that are hard for you.

Spelling Patterns

e	ea	ai	ay
dr**e**ss	h**ea**d	s**ai**d	s**ay**s

Spelling and Meaning

Clues   Write the spelling word for each clue.

1. includes a ZIP code _____
2. once more _____
3. what is done to a book _____
4. opposite of *remember* _____
5. used your money _____
6. all set _____
7. aid _____
8. I say, you say, he ___ _____

Classifying   Write the spelling word that belongs in each group.

9. hour   minute _____
10. exam   quiz _____
11. spoke   told _____
12. first   then _____
13. stop   quit _____
14. blouse   skirt _____
15. toast   juice _____

Word Story   The phrase "raining cats and dogs" is called an **idiom**. In an idiom, the meanings of the words don't add up to the meaning of the phrase. Write the spelling word that completes each idiom below.

He **kept his** ___ when he got lost.

Don't **lose your** ___ during a storm.

16. _____

Family Tree: *help*   Think about how the *help* words are alike in spelling and meaning. Then add another *help* word to the tree.

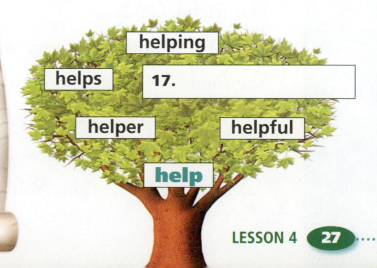

helping

helps   17.

helper   helpful

help

ME-2

ME-2 was a little robot with a big problem. She had a very bad memory. On Friday morning ME-2 ate bread and a scrambled _____₁. Then she forgot that she had eaten breakfast, so she ate it _____₂. On Saturday morning she put on blue jeans. Then she forgot what she had planned to wear, so she put on her best _____₃, too.

Things were bad at home. They were no better at school. When her teacher asked her a question about a story, ME-2 forgot what she had _____₄. When the teacher gave the class a _____₅, ME-2 had forgotten to study for it. She couldn't find her pencil, either. She was never _____₆ for gym because she always forgot her sneakers.

One day ME-2 forgot where she lived. She had forgotten her own _____₇! ME-2 _____₈ the night with her best friend, US-2.

ME-2's mother was very worried. She found ME-2 at school early the very _____₉ day. ME-2's mother _____₁₀, "This won't happen a _____₁₁ time. You are going to the doctor."

next
egg
says
ready
end
help
spent
again
second
forget
dress
said
address
read
test
head

The doctor gave ME-2 a checkup. Soon it was over.
ME-2 told her mother, "The doctor _____
12
I'm just fine. I wish I could remember why you brought
me here."

"Doctor, how can ME-2 be fine?" asked her mother.
"She would lose her _____ if it was not screwed
13
on her shoulders! Can't you _____ her?"
14

The mother's words gave the doctor an idea. He looked
at the screws in ME-2's head. Sure enough, one screw was
loose. He fixed it. That put an _____ to
15
ME-2's bad memory.

"Oh, no! I just remembered something," cried ME-2.
"We get report cards tomorrow. That is something I wish
I could _____!"
16

Spelling and Writing

next
egg
says
ready
end
help
spent
again
second
forget
dress
said
address
read
test
head

Write to the Point

Sometimes it may be hard to remember all the things you have to do every day. You can help yourself remember by making a list. Make a list of things you have to do before and after school every day. Try to use spelling words from this lesson in your list.

Use the strategies on page 7 when you are not sure how to spell a word.

Proofreading

Proofread the journal entry below. Use proofreading marks to correct five spelling mistakes, two capitalization mistakes, and three punctuation mistakes.

Proofreading Marks

◯ spell correctly
≡ capitalize
⊙ add period

October 18

Today I forgot to take my lunch to school.

I often forgit things Mom sezs that i need to

use my hed. she gave me some string

and told me about a trick that

will healp I will use the string

to tie a bow around my

secund finger The bow will help

me remember my lunch.

Dictionary Skills

Multiple Meanings   Many words have more than one meaning. If an entry word in a dictionary has more than one meaning, the different meanings are numbered. Read the dictionary entry below.

> **then** (*thĕn*) *adverb* **1.** At the time: *I used to sleep with a teddy bear, but I was only a baby then.* **2.** After that: *We saw lightning flash, and then we heard the thunder roar.* **3.** A time mentioned: *Go finish your homework, and by then dinner will be ready.*

1. What is the entry word? _____

2. How many meanings does the word have? _____

Write the words *egg, address, next,* and *help* in alphabetical order. Then look them up in the Spelling Dictionary. Write the page on which each entry appears. Then write the number of meanings each word has.

Word	Page	Number of Meanings
3. _____	_____	_____
4. _____	_____	_____
5. _____	_____	_____
6. _____	_____	_____

Challenge Yourself

What do you think each Challenge Word means? Check the Spelling Dictionary to see if you are right. Then use separate paper to write sentences showing that you understand the meaning of each Challenge Word.

Challenge Words

genuine
athletic
attempt
celebration

7. ME-2 was a **genuine** robot.

8. She liked gym class because she was **athletic**.

9. The doctor's first **attempt** to help ME-2 did not work.

10. They had a **celebration** when ME-2 got a good report card.

Lesson 5

Plural Words

apples

1. -s Plurals

_____

_____

_____

_____

_____

_____

_____

_____

_____

_____

_____

_____

2. -es Plurals

_____

_____

_____

_____

tests

pages

papers

dresses

hammers

tables

clowns

classes

paints

apples

eggs

matches

hands

trains

addresses

places

Say and Listen

Say the spelling words. Listen for the ending sounds.

Think and Sort

All of the spelling words are plural words. **Plural** words name more than one thing. Most plural words are formed by adding -s.

boy + **s** = boy**s**   page + **s** = page**s**

Singular words name one thing. If a singular word ends in _s_, _ss_, _ch_, or _x_, -_es_ is added to form the plural.

glass + **es** = glass**es**

1. Write the **twelve** spelling words that are formed by adding -_s_.

2. Write the **four** spelling words that are formed by adding -_es_.

Use the steps on page 6 to study words that are hard for you.

Spelling Patterns

-s	-es
test**s**	dress**es**
page**s**	

Spelling and Meaning

Making Connections Complete each sentence with the spelling word that goes with the workers.

1. Artists use brushes and _____.

2. Carpenters work with nails and _____.

3. Fruit farmers grow oranges and _____.

4. Cooks work with milk and _____.

5. Teachers grade projects and _____.

6. Writers work with _____ in books.

7. Tailors sew skirts and _____.

8. Mail carriers work with names and _____.

Definitions Write the spelling word for each definition. Use the Spelling Dictionary if you need to.

9. questions that measure knowledge   _____

10. small sticks of wood used to light fires   _____

11. connected railroad cars   _____

12. part of the arms below the wrists   _____

13. particular areas   _____

14. circus performers who make people laugh   _____

15. groups of students taught by the same teacher   _____

Word Story One spelling word comes from the Latin word *tabula*. A *tabula* was a board or plank. The spelling word that comes from *tabula* names things on which we set our food or play games. Write the word.

16. _____

Family Tree: *hands* *Hands* is a form of *hand*. Think about how the *hand* words are alike in spelling and meaning. Then add another *hand* word to the tree.

handle

hands

17.

handful

handy

hand

Behind the Scenes

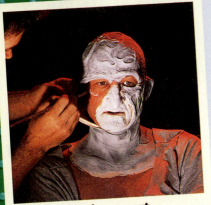
makeup art

When many people think of movie artists, they think of actors. Actors are important movie artists. But other kinds of movie artists are important, too.

Makeup artists work on the actors. They make the actors look like the characters the actors are playing. Makeup artists brush face _____ onto actors
1
to make them look funny, scary, or old. These artists may also use makeup on actors' arms and _____. They do this so that
2
all of the skin looks the same.

Costume artists plan and help make the clothes actors wear. These include fancy gowns and other kinds of _____ from the past.
3
Costume artists also make silly baggy pants for actors who play circus _____. They even make animal costumes for actors to wear.
4

Other movie artists make the movie sets, or the _____ where the stories take
5
place. They use saws, wood, _____,
6
and nails to make rooms. They build the rooms inside larger rooms called studios. They also build _____, chairs, and other pieces of
7
furniture for the set.

set builder

Prop artists find the objects actors need. For example, a movie script may say that actors eat fruit in one part of the movie. A prop artist must find shiny red _____ .
                                                                                8

In another part of the movie, an actor may have to light a fire. A prop artist must have wood and _____
                                                                                9
on hand.

Other artists work with special sounds in movies. A movie may call for the sound of _____ frying. A sound
                                                                                10
artist might crumple _____ to make the sound.
                                11
Another part of the movie might call for the sound of two

_____ racing down a railroad track. A sound
12
artist might use a recording of real trains. A sound artist puts all sounds through several different _____ to
                                                                                13
make sure they sound real.

Would you like to be a movie artist? You can start by working on school plays. You can take special

_____ , too. You can also look in the yellow
14

_____ of the telephone book. Find the
15

_____ and telephone numbers of
16
children's theaters near you. Get behind the scenes!

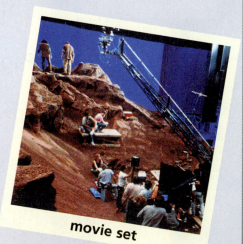
movie set

tests
pages
papers
dresses
hammers
tables
clowns
classes
paints
apples
eggs
matches
hands
trains
addresses
places

Spelling and Writing

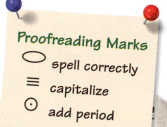

Write to the Point

Many people enjoy movies. Write an ad telling people about a movie. The movie can be a real one or one you make up. Include details that will make people want to see the movie. Try to use spelling words from this lesson.

Use the strategies on page 7 when you are not sure how to spell a word.

Proofreading

Proofread the movie review below. Use proofreading marks to correct five spelling mistakes, three capitalization mistakes, and two punctuation mistakes.

Spelling list

tests
pages
papers
dresses
hammers
tables
clowns
classes
paints
apples
eggs
matches
hands
trains
addresses
places

Proofreading Marks

◯ spell correctly

≡ capitalize

⊙ add period

MOVIE REVIEW

Do you like funny movies? If you do, you will love *Pagess from Our Lives*. it is the story of a group of clownes as they travel to different playces all over the world They use apples and egges to teach juggling to children at a school in France. they also dance on tabels at a park in China. you will have a great time at this movie Your parents will like it, too.

Dictionary Skills

Base Words   A base word is a word from which other words are formed. For example, *apple* is the base word in *apples*, and *test* is the base word in *tests*.

Many entry words in a dictionary are base words. Different forms of a base word may be listed in the entry. The different forms are printed in dark type. Look up the word *dress* in the Spelling Dictionary. How many different forms of *dress* does the entry show? What are they?

Write the following words in alphabetical order. Write the base word for each word. Then find the base word in the Spelling Dictionary. Write the number of different forms given for the word.

hands   **addresses**   **trains**   **pages**   **paints**

Word	Base Word	Number of Word Forms
1. _____	_____	_____
2. _____	_____	_____
3. _____	_____	_____
4. _____	_____	_____
5. _____	_____	_____

Challenge Yourself

Write the Challenge Word for each clue. Use the Spelling Dictionary to see if you are right. Then use separate paper to write sentences showing that you understand the meaning of each Challenge Word.

Challenge Words

losses	meteors
caverns	neckties

6. These look like bright streaks of light in the sky.   _____

7. This word is made from two shorter words put together.

   _____

8. These can make ball players sad.   _____

9. You might find bats in these.   _____

Unit 1 Review
Lessons 1–5

Use the steps on page 6 to study words that are hard for you.

1
subtract
catch
January
half
laugh

Words with Short *a*

Write the spelling word that completes each analogy.

1. *Grab* is to _____ as *pitch* is to *throw*.
2. *Ten* is to *five* as *whole* is to _____.
3. *Chuckle* is to _____ as *cry* is to *sob*.
4. *Multiply* is to *divide* as *add* is to _____.
5. *Snow* is to _____ as *rain* is to *April*.

2
place
gray
break
great
April

Words with Long *a*

Write the spelling word that belongs in each group.

6. February, March, _____
7. put, set, _____
8. wonderful, excellent, _____
9. green, yellow, _____
10. crack, split, _____

3
afraid
danger
table
weigh
they

More Words with Long *a*

Write the spelling word for each clue.

11. something you should try to avoid _____
12. how people want you to feel when they yell "Boo!" _____

13. a word that can be used to name others

_____

14. what scales are used for _____

15. what you set before a meal and sit at to

eat the meal _____

4 Words with Short e

address
second
ready
again
says

Write the spelling word that completes each sentence.

16. Are you _____ for school?

17. If my hair is still messy, I need to comb

it _____.

18. My mother _____, "Clean up
your room, please."

19. At the end of the race, Mario was in

_____ place.

20. Your street, town, and ZIP code are parts

of your _____.

5 Plural Words

eggs
hammers
places
apples
matches

Write the spelling word that answers each question.

21. What are red, round, and juicy? _____

22. What do hens lay? _____

23. What tools are good for pounding nails?

_____

24. Which word rhymes with *spaces*?

_____

25. What can be used to light fires?

_____

26. /ă/ Words

_____
_____
_____
_____
_____

27. /ā/ Words

_____
_____
_____
_____
_____
_____
_____
_____
_____

28. /ĕ/ Words

_____
_____
_____
_____
_____

Review Sort

half	they	second	afraid
break	danger	gray	place
table	catch	says	again
great	ready	January	laugh
eggs	weigh	subtract	

26. Write the **five** short *a* words. Circle the letters that spell /ă/ in each word.

27. Write the **nine** long *a* words. Circle the letters that spell /ā/ in each word.

28. Write the **five** short *e* words. Circle the letters that spell /ĕ/ in each word.

These four words have been sorted into two groups. Explain how the words in each group are alike.

29. hammers   places

_____
_____

30. dresses   matches

_____
_____

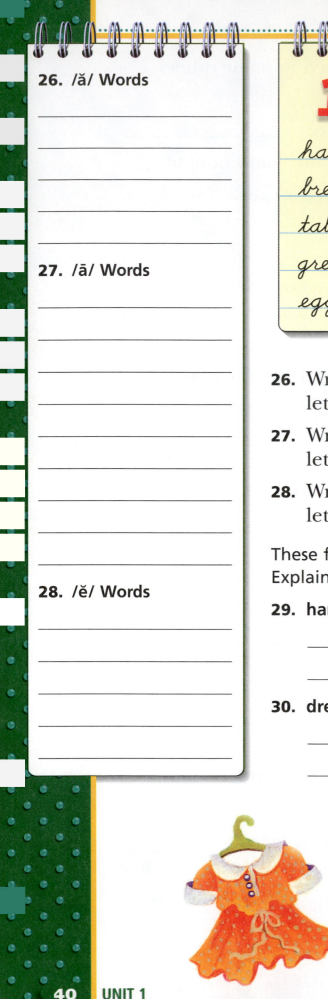

Writer's Workshop

A Personal Narrative

A personal narrative is a true story about the writer. This kind of writing contains words like *I*, *me*, *my*, and *mine*. Here is part of Maria's personal narrative about her first job.

Prewriting To write her personal narrative, Maria followed the steps in the writing process. After she decided on a topic, she used a chain of events chart to list the things that happened. The chart helped Maria tell the story events in the right order. Part of Maria's chain of events chart is shown here. Study what Maria did.

My First Job
My first job taught me a big lesson. One day Ms. Chen offered me ten dollars. All I had to do was carry some magazines and newspapers from her basement to a trash can in her yard. "Great!" I said.

1
Ms. Chen offered me $10 to carry magazines.

2
She showed me her huge basement full of magazines.

3
The job took two weeks.

It's Your Turn!

Write your own personal narrative. It can be about the first time you did something, such as your first day of school or your first soccer game. After you have decided on your topic, make a chain of events chart. Then follow the other steps in the writing process—writing, revising, proofreading, and publishing. Try to use spelling words from this lesson in your personal narrative.

More Words with Short *e*

cents

1. *e* Words

_____
_____
_____
_____
_____
_____
_____
_____
_____
_____
_____
_____
_____

2. *ie* Word

_____

3. *a* Word

_____

4. *ue* Word

_____

slept
February
them
never
when
many
sent
kept
September
best
friend
then
cents
Wednesday
guess
better

Say and Listen

Say each spelling word. Listen for the short e sound.

Think and Sort

Look at the letters in each word. Think about how short e is spelled. Spell each word aloud.

Short e can be shown as /ĕ/. How many spelling patterns for /ĕ/ do you see?

1. Write the **thirteen** spelling words that have the *e* pattern.

2. Write the **one** spelling word that has the *ie* pattern.

3. Write the **one** spelling word that has the *a* pattern.

4. Write the **one** spelling word that has the *ue* pattern.

Use the steps on page 6 to study words that are hard for you.

Spelling Patterns

e	ie	a	ue
b**e**st	fr**ie**nd	m**a**ny	g**ue**ss

Spelling and Meaning

Classifying   Write the spelling word that belongs in each group.

1. lots   several   _____
2. pal   buddy   _____
3. July   August   _____
4. Monday   Tuesday   _____
5. rested   napped   _____
6. December   January   _____
7. good   better   _____
8. mailed   shipped   _____
9. who   what   _____

Rhymes   Write the spelling word that completes each sentence and rhymes with the underlined word.

10. If you don't have a <u>pen</u>, _____ I will lend you one.

11. No one <u>slept</u> because the dog _____ us up.

12. Tell _____ to <u>hem</u> the curtains.

13. Have you ever read a _____ <u>letter</u>?

14. Let me _____ who made this <u>mess</u>.

15. I _____ knew you were so <u>clever</u>.

Word Story   The Latin word *centum* meant "hundred." Several English words come from *centum*. A *century* is one hundred years. A *centipede* is an animal with one hundred legs. Write the spelling word that means "hundredths of a dollar."

16. _____

Family Tree: *friend*   Think about how the *friend* words are alike in spelling and meaning. Then add another *friend* word to the tree.

friendless

friendly

17.

friends

friend

Lily

It was the month of _____,
1
so it was very cold in New Jersey. Lan and
her family were going to sunny Florida on
_____. Before they left, Lan took
2
her pet frog to Carlos. "I'm so glad you are going to take care of
Lily for me," she told him. "This frog is the _____
3
pet I've ever had. Take her home in this shoebox. I'll pick her up
on Saturday."

"This is great! I like frogs," said Carlos. He took the shoebox
home. But when he opened it, Lily jumped out. Carlos looked
for a long time, but he couldn't find Lily anywhere in the house.
"I'll _____ find Lily," he groaned. "I guess I should
4
have _____ the box closed."
5
Carlos went to bed worried about Lily. That night while he
_____, he dreamed about Lily. He woke up even more
6
worried. At school that day, he told his _____ Cody
7
what had happened. "Lan is coming back in two days. I have to
find Lily by _____," Carlos said in a shaky voice.
8
Cody said, "I have a _____ idea. Let's go to the
9
pet store and buy another frog. Lan will never _____
10
that it's not Lily."

The pet store had _____ frogs. Carlos
                        11
and Cody looked at _____ all. They found
                        12
one that looked just like Lily.

"Five dollars," said the sales clerk.

"We have only sixty _____," said Carlos
                              13
sadly. The clerk _____ the boys away.
                        14

On Saturday morning Lan came to get Lily. Carlos
opened the door. He didn't know what to say. Suddenly
he heard a croak. Lily jumped out of his jacket pocket.

"Lily!" cried Lan happily. "Thanks for taking such
good care of her, Carlos. Would you take care of her
again _____ we visit my grandmother in
              15
_____?"
      16
Carlos looked at Lily and smiled.

slept
February
them
never
when
many
sent
kept
September
best
friend
then
cents
Wednesday
guess
better

Spelling and Writing

Word List
slept
February
them
never
when
many
sent
kept
September
best
friend
then
cents
Wednesday
guess
better

Write to the Point

People often put up signs when they lose a pet. Make a sign that Carlos could have used when Lily was lost. Describe Lily, tell when she was lost, and give a phone number to call. You can even offer a reward. Try to use spelling words from this lesson in your sign.

> Use the strategies on page 7 when you are not sure how to spell a word.

Proofreading

Proofread the e-mail below. Use proofreading marks to correct five spelling mistakes, three capitalization mistakes, and two punctuation mistakes.

Proofreading Marks
◯ spell correctly
≡ capitalize
? add question mark

---

e-mail

| Address Book | Attachment | Check Spelling | Send | Save Draft | Cancel |

Ben,

My frend Kim has two goldfish named Spike and Mike. She keeps thim in a big fishbowl. Last february Kim went to texas to visit her grandmother. Can you gess what I did I kep her fish at my house. They were fun to watch and take care of. kim was happy that her fish were safe. Can I watch your fish in Saptember

Your friend,

Gwen

Language Connection

Capital Letters Use a capital letter to begin the names of people and pets and to write the word *I*. Also use a capital letter to begin the first word of a sentence.

The following sentences have capitalization errors. Write each sentence correctly.

1. the book i like best was written by fred gibson.

   _____

2. it is about a dog called old yeller.

   _____

3. travis and old yeller have many adventures.

   _____

4. carl anderson wrote about a horse named blaze.

   _____

5. blaze was kept by a boy named billy.

   _____

6. a horse named thunderbolt became friends with billy and blaze.

   _____

Challenge Yourself

Challenge Words

sketch
index
blend
friendliness

Write the Challenge Word for each clue. Check the Spelling Dictionary to see if you are right. Then use separate paper to write sentences showing that you understand the meaning of each Challenge Word.

7. When you do this, you mix things.

   _____

8. This makes people feel liked. _____

9. You can use this to find something in a book. _____

10. It helps to do this before you make a final drawing. _____

Words with Long *e*

read

1. ee Words

_____
_____
_____
_____
_____
_____
_____
_____

2. ea Words

_____
_____
_____
_____
_____
_____
_____

3. eo Word

_____

street
please
free
wheel
read
queen
each
sneeze
people
meet
team
sea
need
dream
sleep
meat

Say and Listen

Say each spelling word. Listen for the long e sound.

Think and Sort

Look at the letters in each word. Think about how long e is spelled. Spell each word aloud.

Long e can be shown as /ē/. How many spelling patterns for /ē/ do you see?

1. Write the **eight** spelling words that have the *ee* pattern.

2. Write the **seven** spelling words that have the *ea* pattern.

3. Write the **one** spelling word that has the *eo* pattern.

Use the steps on page 6 to study words that are hard for you.

Spelling Patterns

ee	ea	eo
m**ee**t	t**ea**m	p**eo**ple

Spelling and Meaning

Analogies   Write the spelling word that completes each analogy.

1. *Sit* is to *chair* as _____ is to *bed*.

2. *Train* is to *track* as *car* is to _____.

3. *Hives* are to *bees* as *houses* are to _____.

4. *Cough* is to *mouth* as _____ is to *nose*.

5. *Book* is to _____ as *movie* is to *watch*.

6. *Rectangle* is to *door* as *circle* is to _____.

7. *Bush* is to *shrub* as *ocean* is to _____.

Definitions   Write the spelling word for each definition. Use the Spelling Dictionary if you need to.

8. food from the flesh of animals   _____

9. a group of people playing on the same side   _____

10. to think, feel, or see during sleep   _____

11. to come together   _____

12. without cost   _____

13. to give pleasure or happiness to   _____

14. every one   _____

15. must have   _____

Word Story   The Old Saxon word *quan* meant "wife." Later it became the Old English word *cwen,* which meant "wife, woman, or wife of the king." What do we say today instead of *cwen?* Write the spelling word.

16. _____

Family Tree: *read*   Think about how the *read* words are alike in spelling and meaning. Then add another *read* word to the tree.

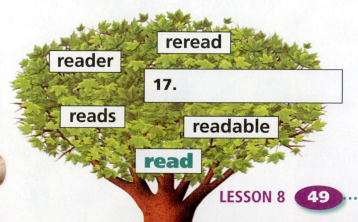

reread

reader

17.

reads

readable

read

Queen of the Roads

Many years ago in a castle by the _____, there lived
                                                          1
a wonderful _____. She was a nice queen. All of the
                          2
_____ in her kingdom loved her. But the queen was not
          3
happy. No one at the castle would let her do any work. Every morning she

had to sit and _____ a book. Every afternoon she had to
                          4
_____ the kings and queens who came to visit. She even
          5
had to eat roasted _____ for every meal.
                                  6
When she went to _____ at night, the queen would
                                  7
often _____ of a different life.
                      8
One morning she woke up early. She told a

servant, "I _____ to get away
                      9
from the castle. I want some time to think.

_____ get a carriage ready
          10
for me."

The servant did as he was asked. In no

time at all, the queen was driving down the

main _____ of the city. "How
                      11
can I be useful?" she asked herself. "What

kind of work can I do?"

The queen traveled far from the castle. The road became bumpy and dusty. She was thinking about being a farmer when her carriage hit a hole in the road. A _____ flew off
₁₂
and got stuck between two large rocks. The queen tried and tried but couldn't get the wheel _____. It was getting
₁₃
dark and cold. She began to shake and _____.
₁₄

At last two farmers came by. "Thank goodness you are here!" said the queen. "Will you help me?"

"Of course!" said the farmers. They helped the queen free the wheel and put it back on the carriage.

"We are a great _____!" said the happy queen.
₁₅
She felt special inside. "How can I thank you?"

"We need new roads that are easy for everyone to travel on," said the farmers.

"New roads you shall have," answered the queen. "And I shall help build _____ and every one!"
₁₆

The queen found a way to be useful. She made many new friends. She stayed busy building new roads with others. After a while everyone began to call her Queen of the Roads. She liked the new name, and she liked her new life. She was never unhappy again.

street
please
free
wheel
read
queen
each
sneeze
people
meet
team
sea
need
dream
sleep
meat

Spelling and Writing

street
please
free
wheel
read
queen
each
sneeze
people
meet
team
sea
need
dream
sleep
meat

Write to the Point

The queen was unhappy because she did not feel useful. She wanted a different kind of life. Write a paragraph about a different kind of life you would like to have. Use descriptive words and details to make your paragraph interesting. Try to use spelling words from this lesson.

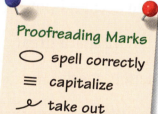

Use the strategies on page 7 when you are not sure how to spell a word.

Proofreading

Proofread the book jacket below. Use proofreading marks to correct five spelling mistakes, three capitalization mistakes, and two unnecessary words.

Proofreading Marks
◯ spell correctly
≡ capitalize
ℯ take out

The Teen Queen

   Readers will love this new story about a young queen. one day she has a a strange dream. In the dream, she is on a baseball teme. each time she gets up to bat, a sea of of peeple cheer her. The queen hits four home runs. after the game, she wants to mete ech fan. Rede this exciting tale to learn what happens when the queen wakes up.

Language Connection

Nouns A noun is a word that names a person, place, thing, or idea. The following words are nouns.

Person	Place	Thing	Idea
boy	seashore	toy	beauty
girl	forest	dog	peace

Write the sentences below, completing them with the correct nouns from the boxes.

meat   wheel   sea   dream   people   street

1. I had a wonderful ___ last night.

_____

2. All the ___ who live on my ___ were in it.

_____

3. I used a big ___ to steer our big ship out to ___.

_____

4. We had a feast of fruit and roasted ___ on an island.

_____

Challenge Yourself

What do you think each Challenge Word means? Check the Spelling Dictionary to see if you are right. Then use separate paper to write sentences showing that you understand the meaning of each Challenge Word.

Challenge Words

deceive	feat
seam	teenager

5. An honest queen does not **deceive** the people in her kingdom.

6. The young knight performed a brave **feat**.

7. I ripped the **seam** in my jacket.

8. I will be a **teenager** when I am thirteen.

More Words with Long *e*

family

1. *e* Word

_____

2. *y* Words

_____

_____

_____

_____

_____

_____

_____

_____

_____

_____

_____

_____

3. *e*-consonant-*e* Word

_____

4. *ey* Word

_____

only
story
key
family
sleepy
carry
sunny
these
funny
very
every
city
penny
even
happy
busy

Say and Listen

Say each spelling word. Listen for the long e sound.

Think and Sort

Look at the letters in each word. Think about how long e is spelled. Spell each word aloud.

Long e can be shown as /ē/. How many spelling patterns for /ē/ do you see?

1. Write the **one** spelling word that has the *e* pattern.

2. Write the **thirteen** spelling words that have the *y* pattern.

3. Write the **one** spelling word that has the *e*-consonant-*e* pattern.

4. Write the **one** spelling word that has the *ey* pattern.

Use the steps on page 6 to study words that are hard for you.

Spelling Patterns

e	y	e-consonant-e	ey
ev**e**n	stor**y**	th**e**s**e**	k**ey**

Spelling and Meaning

Definitions   Write the spelling word for each definition.
Use the Spelling Dictionary if you need to.

1. to take from one place to another   _____

2. extremely   _____

3. the most important part   _____

4. laughable   _____

5. each   _____

6. one cent   _____

7. nearby items   _____

8. a telling of something that happened   _____

9. just   _____

Antonyms   Write the spelling word that is an antonym
of the underlined word.

10. Seth was <u>sad</u> when summer camp began.   _____

11. We will go to the zoo on a <u>cloudy</u> day.   _____

12. Saturday was a <u>lazy</u> day for everyone.   _____

13. Life in the <u>country</u> can be very exciting.   _____

14. Kara felt <u>lively</u> after reading a book.   _____

15. Twelve is an <u>odd</u> number.   _____

Word Story   Long ago in Rome, rich people had servants. The servants were called *familia*. As time passed, a husband, wife, their children, and their servants were called a *familia*. What spelling word comes from *familia*? Write the word.

16. _____

Family Tree: *happy*   Think about how the *happy* words are alike in spelling and meaning. Then add another *happy* word to the tree.

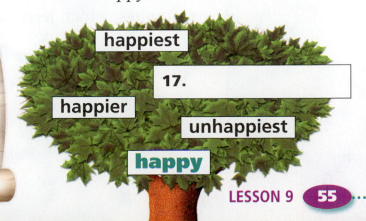

happiest

17.

happier

unhappiest

happy

Use each spelling word once to complete the selection.

The Best Job in the World

Do you like to draw? The artist Jerry Pinkney loved to draw when he was a child. Today he draws pictures for children's books.

Jerry Pinkney was born in 1939. He grew up in the _____ of Philadelphia, **1** Pennsylvania. There were six children in his

_____. The Pinkneys were not rich. They had to **2** watch every _____. **3**

Jerry was a pleasant and _____ child. He spent **4** a lot of time with his aunts, uncles, and cousins. One year an aunt and uncle bought a farm. During the summer the whole family gathered there on weekends. Jerry and his cousins helped the grownups build a house. They had outdoor cookouts on warm, _____ days. When the children grew tired **5** and _____ at night, they slept under the stars. **6**

Young Jerry liked to draw _____ much. An **7** artist friend, John Liney, wanted to help him. Liney gave Jerry art supplies, which Jerry would _____ home. **8**

Even though Jerry was _____ 9 _____ 11 years old, he knew he wanted to be an artist.

In high school Jerry took _____ 10 _____ art class the school offered. He _____ 11 _____ went to night school. After high school Jerry studied art in college for more than two years.

After college Jerry worked as a truck driver and as a designer in a flower shop. He knew that _____ 12 _____ jobs were not right for him. He kept drawing in his spare time. Jerry never gave up his dream. Never giving up may have been the _____ 13 _____ to his later success.

Soon Jerry got a job designing greeting cards. Then he got the chance to draw pictures for a book. The book was a _____ 14 _____ that retold an African folk tale. Jerry has been _____ 15 _____ drawing for stories and books ever since.

Today Jerry Pinkney is a famous artist and lives in the state of New York. He has drawn pictures for many books. Some are serious books, such as *Home Place*. Others are _____ 16 _____ books, such as *Sam and the Tigers*. Pinkney also teaches young people to draw. He likes sharing his talent and skill with others. Some people think he has the best job in the world.

*only
story
key
family
sleepy
carry
sunny
these
funny
very
every
city
penny
even
happy
busy*

Spelling and Writing

Write to the Point

Jerry Pinkney wanted to be an artist when he grew up. What would you like to be? Write a paragraph about a job that you would like to have someday. Use spelling words from this lesson.

Use the strategies on page 7 when you are not sure how to spell a word.

Proofreading

Proofread the letter below. Use proofreading marks to correct five spelling mistakes, three capitalization mistakes, and two punctuation mistakes.

Proofreading Marks
- ◯ spell correctly
- ≡ capitalize
- ⊙ add period

Spelling word list:
- only
- story
- key
- family
- sleepy
- carry
- sunny
- these
- funny
- very
- every
- city
- penny
- even
- happy
- busy

306 Maple Drive

Campbell, CA 95011

November 10, 2003

Dear Tina,

My mom got a new job. she is going to be a firefighter

in the big citty of Chicago, Illinois Our familee is very hapy.

we have been buzy packing since early thursday morning I will

write again verry soon and tell you more.

Your cousin,

Tasha

Dictionary Skills

Alphabetical Order   The words in a dictionary are in alphabetical order. Use the Spelling Dictionary to complete the following sentences.

1. Words that begin with **A** start on page _____ and

    end on page _____ .

2. Words that begin with **M** start on page _____ and

    end on page _____ .

3. Words that begin with **W** start on page _____ and

    end on page _____ .

Write the words below in alphabetical order. Then find each one in the Spelling Dictionary and write its page number.

| funny | even | carry | key |

Word	**Page**
4. _____	_____
5. _____	_____
6. _____	_____
7. _____	_____

Challenge Yourself

What do you think each Challenge Word means? Check the Spelling Dictionary to see if you are right. Then use separate paper to write sentences showing that you understand the meaning of each Challenge Word.

Challenge Words

misery   scheme
soggy   cemetery

8. A headache can cause **misery**.

9. The children had a **scheme** for raising money to buy a gift.

10. Mia changed her **soggy** clothes after she fell in a puddle.

11. Some grave markers in this **cemetery** are very old.

Words with Short *u*

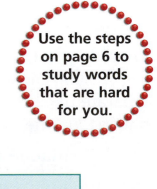

summer

1. *u* Words

_____
_____
_____
_____
_____
_____
_____

2. *o* Words

_____
_____
_____
_____
_____
_____
_____
_____

3. *oe* Word

_____

from
Sunday
money
under
nothing
summer
does
mother
lunch
month
such
front
much
sun
other
Monday

Say and Listen

Say each spelling word. Listen for the short *u* sound.

Think and Sort

Look at the letters in each word. Think about how short *u* is spelled. Spell each word aloud.

Short *u* can be shown as /ŭ/. How many spelling patterns for /ŭ/ do you see?

1. Write the **seven** spelling words that have the *u* pattern.

2. Write the **eight** spelling words that have the *o* pattern.

3. Write the **one** spelling word that has the *oe* pattern.

Use the steps on page 6 to study words that are hard for you.

Spelling Patterns

u	o	oe
s**u**n	m**o**nth	d**oe**s

Letter Scramble   Unscramble the underlined letters to make a spelling word. Write the word on the line.

1. Kelly was at the <u>tronf</u> of the line.   _____

2. We hid the keys <u>drune</u> the mat.   _____

3. How much <u>noemy</u> is in your pocket?   _____

4. We had never seen <u>chus</u> a mess.   _____

5. We could see <u>honnitg</u> in the dark.   _____

6. When <u>osde</u> the bus come?   _____

Clues   Write the spelling word for each clue.

7. The first one is January.   _____

8. This day comes before Tuesday.   _____

9. This word is the opposite of *to*.   _____

10. When it shines, you feel warmer.   _____

11. This day comes after Saturday.   _____

12. This person has at least one son or daughter.   _____

13. If you have this, you have a lot.   _____

14. This season contains June, July, and August.   _____

15. This word means "different."   _____

Word Story   You probably use this spelling word every day. It comes from the old English word *nuncheon,* which meant "a light meal." Later *nuncheon* changed to *luncheon* and also meant "a thick piece." The spelling word names the meal you eat at noon. Write the word.

16. _____

Family Tree: *does*   *Does* is a form of *do*. Think about how the *do* words are alike in spelling and meaning. Then add another *do* word to the tree.

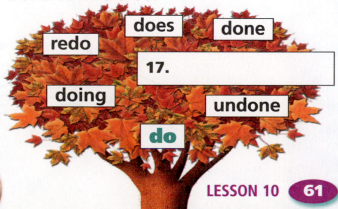

does   done
redo
17.
doing
undone
do

Facing the Music

It was June, the last _____ of school. It was also the
1
last weekend before _____ vacation. Josh's favorite day
2
was _____, but not this Sunday.
3

On Saturday Josh found ten dollars in his jacket. He could not
remember where the _____ came _____.
4   5
But he knew how _____ he wanted a compact disc, so
6
he bought it with the money.

This morning he remembered how he got the money. The ten
dollars was class money. The _____ students had given
7
him the money to buy a present for Mr. Farar, their music teacher.
Josh didn't have any more money, and the compact disc had been on
sale. He couldn't return it.

Josh was upset. His _____ asked what was wrong.
8
"It's _____," he told her. He couldn't bring himself to
9
tell her about his mistake.

Then Petra called and asked, "How _____
10
Mr. Farar's present look?"

"Well . . . ," Josh began.

"Remember to put a note on it. Don't forget all of our names."

Josh hung up the telephone. Petra's words had given him a great idea. He found his modeling clay _____ 11 his bed. He formed the clay into an egg shape and stuck a stick into it. Josh dried the whole thing outside in the _____ 12. Then he painted it silver. When the paint was dry, he added all the students' names.

By _____ 13 morning all the names were dry. Josh wrapped the gift and took it to school. At noon he went to _____ 14. Petra asked, "Where are the present and the note?"

"You'll see," said Josh.

Mr. Farar opened his gift in _____ 15 of the class. "Wow! A compact disc and a silver music note with your names on it!" he exclaimed. "This note took _____ 16 a lot of work. Thank you! It's one note I'll hold forever!"

from
Sunday
money
under
nothing
summer
does
mother
lunch
month
such
front
much
sun
other
Monday

Spelling and Writing

Write to the Point

Josh made a gift for Mr. Farar out of clay. Think of a gift you can make out of things you have at home or school. Then write a paragraph telling what the gift is and how to make it. Try to use spelling words from this lesson.

Use the strategies on page 7 when you are not sure how to spell a word.

Proofreading

Proofread the e-mail message below. Use proofreading marks to correct five spelling mistakes, three capitalization mistakes, and two punctuation mistakes.

Proofreading Marks

◯ spell correctly
≡ capitalize
? add question mark

---

e-mail

| Address Book | Attachment | Check Spelling | Send | Save Draft | Cancel |

Dear Grandpa,

Thank you for the soccer ball and mony you gave

me for my birthday on Munday. Somer begins in only

one more month. Can you believe it I am going to play

soccer in our frunt yard every day. each sunday I will

come to your house. We can sit in the sun and eat

lonch. We'll have fun! does that sound good to you

Josh

ANA JOSH PETRA KIM

Language Connection

Question Marks Use a question mark at the end of a sentence that asks a question.

> Do you like riddles? Can you answer these?

your teeth

your lap

the letter m

Write each riddle correctly. Then choose one of the answers in the boxes and write it in the space provided.

1. What comes once in a month, twice in a moment, but never in a hundred years

   _____

   _____

   Answer: _____

2. What do you lose whenever you stand up

   _____

   Answer: _____

3. What can you put into the apple pie you have for lunch

   _____

   Answer: _____

Challenge Yourself

Write the Challenge Word for each clue. Check the Spelling Dictionary to see if you are right. Then use separate paper to write sentences showing that you understand the meaning of each Challenge Word.

Challenge Words

huddle   buzzard
somebody frontier

4. We use this word to talk about a person we don't know. _____

5. This is a large bird with a beak. _____

6. This is a place where few people live. _____

7. Football players make one of these to plan their next move.

   _____

Contractions

they'll

will Contractions

1. will Contractions
_____
_____
_____
_____
_____

2. have Contractions
_____
_____
_____
_____

3. would or had Contractions
_____
_____
_____

4. is or has Contractions
_____
_____
_____

5. am Contraction
_____

Spelling words:

she's
they'll
I've
you'll
we've
I'm
I'll
you've
it's
I'd
you'd
we'll
they'd
she'll
they've
he's

Say and Listen

Say the spelling words. Listen to the ending sounds.

Think and Sort

Each spelling word is a **contraction**. Two words are joined, but one or more letters are left out. An apostrophe (') is used in place of the missing letters.

Had and *would* are written the same way in contractions. So are *is* and *has*.

1. Write the **five** spelling words that are *will* contractions.

2. Write the **four** spelling words that are *have* contractions.

3. Write the **three** spelling words that are *would* or *had* contractions.

4. Write the **three** spelling words that are *is* or *has* contractions.

5. Write the **one** spelling word that is an *am* contraction.

Use the steps on page 6 to study words that are hard for you.

Spelling Patterns

will	have	would/had	is/has	am
we'll	you've	they'd	she's	I'm

Spelling and Meaning

Trading Places   Write the contraction that could be used instead of the underlined words in each sentence.

1. It <u>is</u> time to eat.   _____

2. I <u>have</u> seen the world's tallest building.   _____

3. He <u>is</u> feeling tired.   _____

4. <u>You will</u> like my uncle's farm.   _____

5. <u>You have</u> grown so tall!   _____

6. <u>They would</u> be happy to see you.   _____

7. <u>They have</u> found their ball.   _____

8. <u>We will</u> make dinner together.   _____

9. <u>We have</u> finished painting.   _____

Rhymes   Write the spelling word that completes each sentence and rhymes with the underlined word.

10. A <u>dime</u> is what _____ looking for.

11. Did you hear Kara <u>sneeze</u>? _____ got a cold.

12. If the children see a <u>whale</u>, _____ be excited.

13. The <u>seal</u> is hungry, so _____ feed it.

14. Let's buy <u>food</u> that _____ like to eat.

15. <u>While</u> you nap, _____ read a book.

Word Story   Verbs have different forms for present, past, and future action. Long ago English verbs had even more forms. A few of these forms are still used today. A special form of the verb *will* used to be spelled *wolde*. Think about how we spell *wolde* today. Then add *I* and write the contraction below.

16. _____

Family Tree: *will*   Think about how the *will* contractions are alike in spelling and meaning. Then add another *will* contraction to the tree.

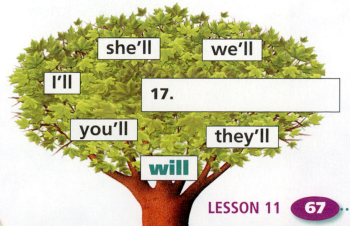

she'll   we'll

I'll

17.

you'll   they'll

will

Diary of a Detective: Case 13

I went over to Riley's house to play. The first thing he did was show me some pork chops. "Look what we are having for dinner," he said with a grin.

I know Riley. _____ always hungry. I'm not.
                         1

_____ rather work on a mystery than eat.
        2

Riley's dad was next door with Mr. Sperry. Riley and I were playing in the back yard. A loud bang came from Riley's house.

"_____ sure that's not Mom," Riley said to me. "I
         3

know _____ still at work. _____ be
            4   5

home in an hour."

Riley and I ran to the house. The back door was wide open. A chair in the kitchen lay on its side. We walked into the hallway. "Look at my coat," I said. "_____ on the
                                                               6

floor!" Then we heard a strange noise upstairs.

"Let's go next door and call the police," Riley whispered to me.

"_____ know what to do. _____
        7   8

handled lots of burglars."

I didn't think it was burglars because _____
9
be quiet. Then I noticed something. "_____ got
10
it!" I yelled.

"Shh!" said Riley. "Be quiet, or _____
11
scare them off!"

"Together _____ be able to handle this,"
12
I said. "_____ got all the clues we need.
13
Look around."

Riley looked. Then he said, "Some of the pork chops are
gone! What kind of burglars would take pork chops? And
look at the floor. Where did those paw prints come from?"

Before I could answer, a puppy came down the stairs.
He barked at us.

Riley laughed. He said, "Well, puppy. I see that
_____ eaten half our dinner. Don't
14
tell me _____ like the rest."
15

The dog just wagged his tail and trotted
out the door. But _____ bet he
16
was happy.

she's
they'll
I've
you'll
we've
I'm
I'll
you've
it's
I'd
you'd
we'll
they'd
she'll
they've
he's

Spelling and Writing

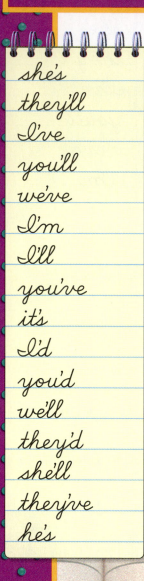

she's
they'll
I've
you'll
we've
I'm
I'll
you've
it's
I'd
you'd
we'll
they'd
she'll
they've
he's

Write to the Point

Think about detectives you know from books or television. Decide what makes these people good detectives. Write a paragraph telling why you or someone you know would be a good detective. Try to use spelling words from this lesson in your paragraph.

Use the strategies on page 7 when you are not sure how to spell a word.

Proofreading

Proofread the journal entry below. Use proofreading marks to correct five spelling mistakes, two capitalization mistakes, and three punctuation mistakes.

Proofreading Marks

◯ spell correctly
≡ capitalize
⊙ add period

November 14

    My friend pete and I found a lost dog today.

I'me not sure whose puppy it is. Pete thought

that I'dd know because I know all the dogs in

the neighborhood He's really worried about the

pup. It's white with black spots.

    Wev' put up signs about finding a lost

puppy. I'v even called Chief collins at the police

station We'l be glad when we find the owner

Language Connection

Contractions At least one letter and sound are missing from every contraction. An apostrophe (') shows where the letter or letters have been left out. For example, in the contraction *we've*, the apostrophe shows that the letters *ha* have been left out.

> I'm = I **a**m   we've = we **ha**ve

Write the contraction for each pair of words. Then write the letter or letters that are left out.

Contraction	Letter or Letters Left Out
1. I will _____	_____
2. he is _____	_____
3. it is _____	_____
4. they have _____	_____
5. you had _____	_____
6. I am _____	_____
7. you would _____	_____
8. she has _____	_____

Challenge Yourself

Use the Spelling Dictionary to look up each Challenge Word. Then answer the questions. Use separate paper to write sentences showing that you understand the meaning of each Challenge Word.

Challenge Words

would've   could've
who'll   where'd

9. Is **would've** a contraction for *would have*? _____

10. Is **could've** a contraction for *could give*? _____

11. Is **who'll** a contraction for *who all*? _____

12. Is **where'd** a contraction for *where did*? _____

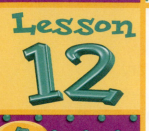

Unit 2 Review
Lessons 7–11

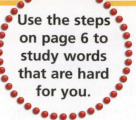

Use the steps on page 6 to study words that are hard for you.

7

Wednesday
February
friend
many
guess

More Words with Short e

Write the spelling word that completes each analogy.

1. *Pal* is to _____ as *chilly* is to *cold*.

2. *Saturday* is to *end* as _____ is to *middle*.

3. *Know* is to *understand* as *suppose* is to _____.

4. *Little* is to *few* as *much* is to _____.

5. *Monday* is to *day* as _____ is to *month*.

8

queen
meet
please
team
people

Words with Long e

Write the spelling word that belongs in each group.

6. duchess   princess   _____

7. group   club   _____

8. persons   humans   _____

9. touch   join   _____

10. delight   cheer   _____

9

even
every
family
these
key

More Words with Long e

Write the spelling word for each clue.

11. This has parents and children.   _____

12. If a floor is flat, it is this.   _____

13. You can use this word instead of *each*.

_____

14. This can unlock a door or start a car.
_____

15. We use this word to point out a group of nearby things. _____

10 Words with Short *u*

lunch
such
other
month
does

Write the spelling word that completes each sentence.

16. My cat always _____ whatever he wants.

17. Mom and Dad pay our bills at the end of the _____.

18. Do you want this blouse or the _____ one?

19. Isaac had soup and a salad for _____ today.

20. Dad and I had never seen _____ a big storm.

11 Contractions

she'll
you've
they'd
it's
I'm

Write the spelling word for each word pair.

21. I am _____

22. you have _____

23. she will _____

24. they would _____

25. it is _____

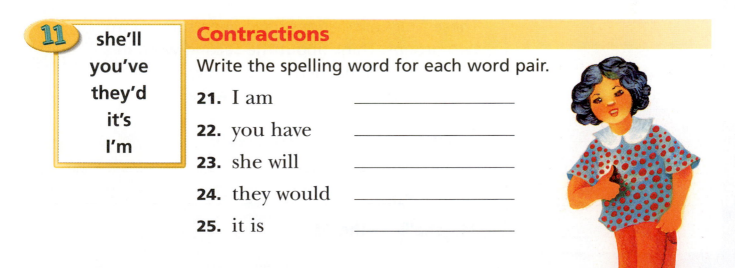

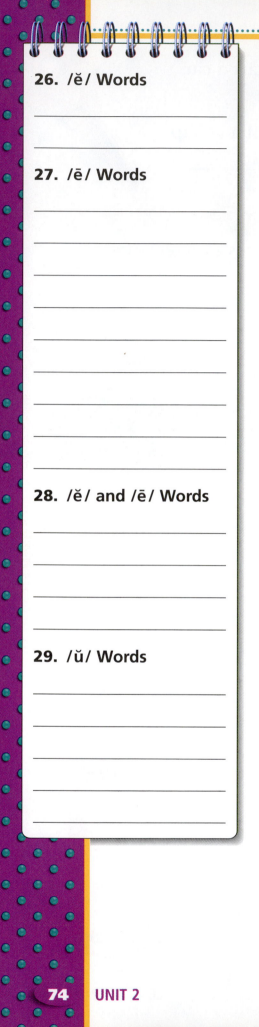

26. /ĕ/ Words

_____

_____

27. /ē/ Words

_____

_____

_____

_____

_____

_____

_____

_____

_____

28. /ĕ/ and /ē/ Words

_____

_____

_____

_____

29. /ŭ/ Words

_____

_____

_____

_____

_____

_____

does	team	month	people
many	February	such	friend
other	please	lunch	these
guess	queen	key	every
meet	Wednesday	family	she'll

26. Write the **two** short *e* words. Circle the letter or letters that spell /ĕ/ in each word.

27. Write the **nine** long *e* words. Circle the letter or letters that spell /ē/ in each word.

28. Write the **four** words that have both /ĕ/ and /ē/.

29. Write the **five** short *u* words. Circle the letter or letters that spell /ŭ/ in each word.

These four contractions have been sorted into two groups. Think about the second word in each contraction. Then explain how the contractions in each group are alike.

30. it's   I'm

_____

_____

31. she'll   they'd

_____

_____

Writer's Workshop

A Narrative

A narrative is a story. Every good story has a beginning, a middle, and an end. In the beginning of a story, writers tell who or what the story is about. They often tell where and when the story takes place. Here is the beginning of Leo's story about an unusual giraffe.

The Mystery of the Talking Giraffe

Ryan looked at Jan. "Did you hear what I heard?" he asked in a trembling voice. Jan didn't answer. She just kept staring at the giraffe. Ryan and Jan lived a block from the Davis City Zoo. They came early every Friday morning, all summer long. The zoo workers knew them by name. Even the animals seemed to recognize them. Still, none of the animals had ever said hello to them before.

Prewriting   To write his narrative, Leo followed the steps in the writing process. After he decided on a topic, he completed a story map. The map helped him decide what would happen at the beginning, middle, and end of his narrative. Leo's story map is shown here. Study what Leo did.

Beginning
Ryan and Jan hear a giraffe say hello.

Middle
They see a wire and speaker.

End
They discover the zookeeper's trick.

It's Your Turn!

Write your own narrative. It can be a mystery like Leo's, an adventure story, or any kind of story you choose. After you have decided on your topic, make a story map. Then follow the other steps in the writing process—writing, revising, proofreading, and publishing. Try to use spelling words from this lesson in your narrative.

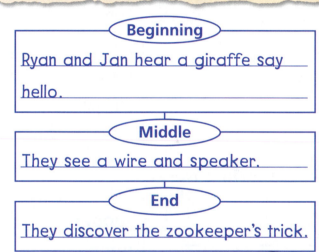

More Words with Short *u*

butter

1. *u* Words

_____
_____
_____
_____
_____
_____
_____

2. *o* Words

_____
_____

3. *o*-consonant-*e* Words

_____
_____
_____
_____
_____
_____
_____

lovely
just
something
hundred
done
some
sum
must
shove
won
butter
cover
supper
none
number
one

Say and Listen

Say each spelling word. Listen for the short *u* sound.

Think and Sort

Look at the letters in each word. Think about how short *u* is spelled. Spell each word aloud.

Short u can be shown as /ŭ/. How many spelling patterns for /ŭ/ do you see?

1. Write the **seven** spelling words that have the *u* pattern.

2. Write the **two** spelling words that have the *o* pattern.

3. Write the **seven** spelling words that have the *o*-consonant-*e* pattern.

Use the steps on page 6 to study words that are hard for you.

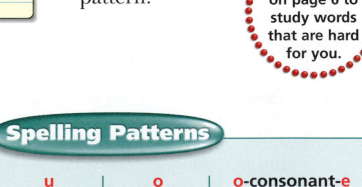

Spelling Patterns

u	o	o-consonant-e
m**u**st	w**o**n	s**o**m**e**
	c**o**v**e**r	

Spelling and Meaning

Definitions   Write the spelling word for each definition.
Use the Spelling Dictionary if you need to.

1. gained a victory   _____
2. to put or lay over   _____
3. a particular thing that is not named   _____
4. a certain number of   _____
5. the answer for an addition problem   _____
6. a number, written 1   _____
7. ten groups of ten   _____
8. will have to   _____
9. amount   _____
10. not any   _____

Synonyms   Complete each sentence by writing the
spelling word that is a synonym for the underlined word.

11. Tan's work will soon be <u>finished</u>.   _____
12. Tasha is wearing a <u>beautiful</u> scarf.   _____
13. I'll <u>push</u> Mother's surprise in the closet.   _____
14. No one could argue with the <u>fair</u> law.   _____
15. Kevin ate fish and rice for <u>dinner</u>.   _____

Word Story   Long ago the
Greek language had the word
boutyron. *Bous* meant "cow." *Tyros*
meant "cheese." The first English
spelling of the word was *butere*.
Write the spelling that we use
today.

16. _____

Family Tree: *cover*   Think about
how the *cover* words are alike in
spelling and meaning. Then add
another *cover* word to the tree.

covered   covering

17. _____

discover   covers

cover

Use each spelling word once to complete the story.

The First Horse Show

Simon rubbed his eyes and then looked out his bedroom window.

"What a _____ day," he thought.
1

"Simon, you _____ get up now. We will be late for the
2

show if you don't," his father called. "We've got a long way to drive, and we

won't be back until it's time for _____."
3

Simon began to feel funny. It felt as though _____ was
4

caught in his throat. He heard his father walking toward his room. He

pulled the blanket up to _____ his head.
5

"Simon, why aren't you up yet?" his father asked from the door.

"I _____ don't think I can do it," Simon replied.
6

"Sure you can," his father said. He smiled and gave Simon a gentle

_____. "Everyone is scared before a show. Even after a
7

_____ shows, you'll still feel that way."
8

Dad could always get Simon going. Simon dressed, grabbed a piece of warm toast, and spread some _____ on it.
9
He knew he would be sorry later if he didn't eat.

Ryan watched his brother. "I want _____ toast,
10
too," he said. Ryan placed two slices of bread in the toaster. He was seven, and he wanted to do everything Simon did.

Simon, his dad, and Ryan loaded their truck and began the trip to the show. For Simon the three-hour trip flew by. After they arrived at the busy arena, Simon signed in. He would be rider _____ ten. "Ten is a great number," he said to
11
himself. "It's the _____ of nine, my age, and
12
_____, for first place."
13

Simon got on his pony, Rocket. They entered the big riding ring. Simon took a deep breath. He and Rocket went to work.

As he finished the jumping course, Simon hoped that _____ of the others had _____
14   15
as well as he and Rocket had.

Simon was still holding his breath when he heard the judge say, "In first place, Simon, riding Rocket."

"Rocket, we _____!" Simon
16
whispered to his horse. "We really won!"

lovely
just
something
hundred
done
some
sum
must
shove
won
butter
cover
supper
none
number
one

1ST PLACE

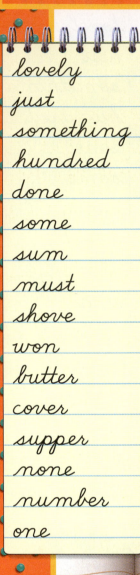

lovely
just
something
hundred
done
some
sum
must
shove
won
butter
cover
supper
none
number
one

Write to the Point

Some people believe that doing your best is more important than winning. Do you agree? Write a paragraph about how important winning is to you. Give reasons why you think as you do. Try to use spelling words from this lesson in your paragraph.

> **Use the strategies on page 7 when you are not sure how to spell a word.**

Proofreading

Proofread the journal entry below. Use proofreading marks to correct five spelling mistakes, three capitalization mistakes, and two punctuation mistakes.

Proofreading Marks
- ◯ spell correctly
- ≡ capitalize
- ⊙ add period

December 15

yesterday was the best day of my life. I jest cannot believe that I won something. rocket and I were nomber one in the show. now we have a lovley ribbon. There were more than two hunderd people watching.

I must enter another horse show soon I've never dun anything as fun as riding in that show. I think Rocket had fun, too. Dad says that he will take us to any show in the state

Language Connection

Homophones   Homophones are words that sound alike but have different spellings and meanings. Look at the homophone pairs in the boxes below. Think about what each homophone means.

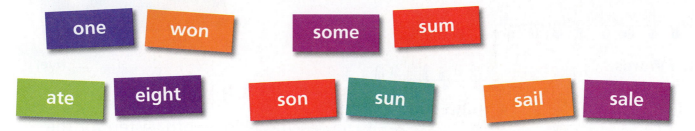

one   won   some   sum
ate   eight   son   sun   sail   sale

Use the homophones above to complete each sentence. Use the Spelling Dictionary if you need to.

1. The ship must _____ at sunrise.

2. I bought this lovely jacket on _____.

3. Jason _____ some soup and a sandwich for supper.

4. My favorite number is _____.

5. The hot _____ made some of us thirsty.

6. We just met Mrs. Lee's daughter and her _____.

7. Jesse _____ two blue ribbons at the art contest.

8. Mr. Ono owns _____ car and two bicycles.

9. Mari found the _____ of _____ numbers.

Challenge Yourself

What do you think each Challenge Word means? Check the Spelling Dictionary to see if you are right. Then use separate paper to write sentences showing that you understand the meaning of each Challenge Word.

Challenge Words	
income	slump
smudge	instruct

10. My allowance is my **income**.

11. The puppy's wet nose left a **smudge** on the window.

12. You will look taller if you don't **slump**.

13. I have a good teacher to **instruct** me in math.

Words with Short *i*

river

1. *i* Words

_____
_____
_____
_____
_____
_____
_____
_____
_____
_____
_____

2. *e* Words

_____
_____

3. *e* and *i* Word

_____

4. *ui* Word

_____

5. *ee* Word

_____

thing
little
winter
kick
begin
river
been
dish
fill
think
spring
pretty
which
December
build
children

Say and Listen

Say each spelling word. Listen for the short *i* sound.

Think and Sort

Look at the letters in each word. Think about how short *i* is spelled. Spell each word aloud.

Short *i* can be shown as /ĭ/. How many spelling patterns for /ĭ/ do you see?

1. Write the **eleven** spelling words that have the *i* pattern.

2. Write the **two** spelling words that have the *e* pattern.

3. Write the **one** spelling word that has the *e* and the *i* patterns.

4. Write the **one** spelling word that has the *ui* pattern.

5. Write the **one** spelling word that has the *ee* pattern.

Use the steps on page 6 to study words that are hard for you.

Spelling Patterns

i	e	ui	ee
d**i**sh	pr**e**tty	b**ui**ld	b**ee**n

Spelling and Meaning

Clues   Write the spelling word for each clue.

1. what you do to a soccer ball   _____

2. young people   _____

3. what you do with a hammer and nails   _____

4. a big stream   _____

5. a season that can be cold   _____

6. a word that rhymes with *fish*   _____

7. the opposite of *end*   _____

8. a word for *beautiful*   _____

9. the opposite of *big*   _____

Rhymes   Write the spelling word that completes each sentence and rhymes with the underlined word.

10. I _____ I will wear my <u>pink</u> shirt.

11. The coach told the player _____ <u>pitch</u> was good.

12. If you have not _____ practicing, you will not <u>win</u> the music contest.

13. I will <u>bring</u> you flowers in the _____.

14. Jill will climb the <u>hill</u> and _____ the bucket.

15. <u>Bring</u> that little blue _____ to me.

Word Story   The Romans of long ago divided the year into ten months. The last Roman month was named *Decem*. *Decem* meant "ten." Write the spelling word that comes from *Decem*.

16. _____

Family Tree: *children*   *Children* is a form of *child*. Think about how the *child* words are alike in spelling and meaning. Then add another *child* word to the tree.

childlike

children

17.

childproof

childless

child

Use each spelling word once to complete the selection.

WESTWARD ADVENTURES

Helen Scott and her family were pioneers. They traveled west across North America when Helen was only 11 years old. Helen and many other pioneers wrote about their adventures in journals, some of _____ we can read today. Their writings have _____ helpful because they tell us about life on the westward trail in the 1800s.

Pioneers traveled west in covered wagons. If a family lived in the middle of the country, the best time to _____ their trip was in the _____, after the rains. The trip took five to six months. A family that left in May could plan to arrive well before the month of _____. That was when the harsh _____ began.

A covered wagon had very _____ room. Families had to _____ carefully about what they would pack. Young _____ could take few toys.

Meals on the trail were simple. Corn mush was a common _____ that most pioneers ate. They also ate dried meat, eggs, and potatoes.

Before dinner, pioneers gathered sticks and branches to _____ a fire for cooking. After dinner, they sang songs around the fire and danced to _____ fiddle music. They told stories, too.

Horses and mules pulled the wagons. The ride was bumpy and uncomfortable. Children often walked beside the slow wagons. They had to be careful. They didn't want the animals to bite or _____ them.

Children worked on the trail, too. Boys and girls helped get the wagons ready to cross any stream or _____. Another _____ children did was to help make a special wax paste to _____ cracks in the covered wagons. Then they helped to fill the openings. Filling the openings helped make the wagons waterproof.

Every day on the westward trail was an adventure. Thanks to children like Helen Scott, we can share those adventures.

thing
little
winter
kick
begin
river
been
dish
fill
think
spring
pretty
which
December
build
children

Spelling and Writing

Write to the Point

Helen Scott was a pioneer who wrote about her adventures. Suppose you are about to travel west and you can only take three things. Write a paragraph that tells the three things you will take with you on your trip. Explain why they are important. Try to use spelling words from this lesson in your paragraph.

Use the strategies on page 7 when you are not sure how to spell a word.

Proofreading

Proofread the postcard below. Use proofreading marks to correct five spelling mistakes, three capitalization mistakes, and two punctuation mistakes.

Proofreading Marks
- ◯ spell correctly
- ≡ capitalize
- ⊙ add period

thing
little
winter
kick
begin
river
been
dish
fill
think
spring
pretty
which
December
build
children

Hi, luke!

We had a great time at the pioneer fair. i saw people buld a barn I learned that it was hard to be a pioneer in the winnter. The rivere freezes by Decembr, and then it is hard to fish. Life is easier when springe comes. maybe you can come to the fair with us next year

Dylan

Luke Babb

158 Beach Drive

Austin, TX 78739

Language Connection

Adjectives   An adjective describes a noun or pronoun by telling which one, what kind, or how many.

| The **spotted** pony ate the **green** grass. | The **fresh** flowers are **lovely**. |

Use the adjectives in the boxes below to complete the sentences. Then circle all the adjectives in the sentences.

icy   little   hot   every   dangerous

pretty   shallow   many   brown   late

1. A river flows by the simple _____ cabin.

2. It travels for _____ miles through the thick forest.

3. In the winter the river is cold and _____.

4. Thin ice in some places is _____ for skaters.

5. Many _____ flowers line the banks in spring.

6. On _____ summer days, people wade in the river.

7. They walk on large rocks in the _____ water.

8. In the fall, red and _____ leaves float down the river.

9. The river changes with _____ season.

Challenge Yourself

Write the Challenge Word for each clue. Check the Spelling Dictionary to see if you are right. Then use separate paper to write sentences showing that you understand the meaning of each Challenge Word.

Challenge Words

| spinach | luggage |
| width | arctic |

10. This word describes very cold air. _____

11. It is a green vegetable. _____

12. This can hold your clothes when you travel. _____

13. It is the distance from one side to another. _____

Words with Long *i*

lion

Notepad

1. *i*-consonant-*e* Words

_____

_____

_____

_____

_____

_____

_____

_____

_____

_____

_____

_____

_____

2. *i* Words

_____

_____

3. *eye* Word

_____

Spelling Words

alike
while
eyes
white
line
lion
size
miles
times
nice
drive
tiny
write
inside
mine
shine

Say and Listen

Say each spelling word. Listen for the long *i* sound.

Think and Sort

Look at the letters in each word. Think about how long *i* is spelled. Spell each word aloud.

Long *i* can be shown as /ī/. How many spelling patterns for /ī/ do you see?

1. Write the **thirteen** spelling words that have the *i*-consonant-*e* pattern.

2. Write the **two** spelling words that have the *i* pattern.

3. Write the **one** spelling word that has the *eye* pattern.

Use the steps on page 6 to study words that are hard for you.

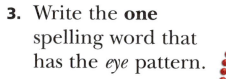

Spelling Patterns

i-consonant-e	i	eye
ni**ce**	t**i**ny	**eye** **eye**s

Spelling and Meaning

Clues   Write the spelling word for each clue.

1. what people do with a car _____
2. belongs in a group with *feet* and *yards* _____
3. something that can be straight or crooked _____
4. a word meaning "at the same time" _____
5. a word that rhymes with *eyes* _____
6. what people do to some shoes _____

Analogies   Write the spelling word that completes each analogy.

7. *Mean* is to _____ as *weak* is to *strong*.
8. *You* is to *me* as *yours* is to _____.
9. *Add* is to *plus* as *multiply* is to _____.
10. *Light* is to *dark* as _____ is to *black*.
11. *Hear* is to *ears* as *see* is to _____.
12. *Needle* is to *sew* as *pen* is to _____.
13. *Small* is to _____ as *big* is to *huge*.
14. *Different* is to *unlike* as *same* is to _____.
15. *Up* is to *down* as _____ is to *outside*.

Word Story   One of the spelling words comes from the Greek word *leon*. *Leon* was the word for one of the big cats. The names Leona, Lenore, Leo, Leopold, and Lionel all come from this word. Write the spelling word that comes from *leon*.

16. _____

Family Tree: *drive*   Think about how the *drive* words are alike in spelling and meaning. Then add another *drive* word to the tree.

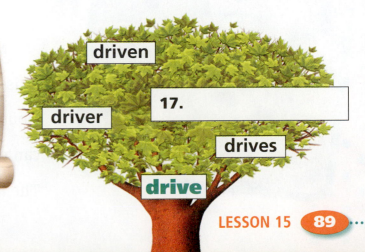

driven

17.

driver

drives

drive

Use each spelling word once
to complete the selection.

Just a Big Cat?

It's easy to tell that a _____
1
belongs to the cat family. A lion looks very

much like a house cat. The two animals are

also _____ in other ways.
2
They both have claws that they can pull

_____ their paws to keep the claws _____
3   4
and sharp. Lions and house cats also have _____ that see
5
well in the dark. If a light should _____ on their eyes at
6
night, their eyes will glow.

Lions are not like house cats in every way.

The greatest difference is _____.
7
A male lion can weigh more than 500 pounds,

_____ a house cat usually
8
weighs about 10 pounds. A house cat seems

_____ next to a lion.
9
Most lions have brownish-yellow fur.

This color makes it easy for the lion to hide.

House cats come in many colors. Their fur

can even be snowy _____.
10
The male lion has a mane. The mane makes

him look big and strong. The thick mane may be why the male lion is called the king of beasts. A male house cat never has a mane.

Lions live in groups called prides. At _____ 11 , as many as 35 lions may live in a pride. These lions hunt together. They may travel many _____ 12 to find food. A lion doesn't let strange animals hunt on its land. The lion will let out a roar as if to say, "Keep out! This land is _____ 13 ."

Today most lions live in Africa, but you can still learn a lot about them. Lions can be seen in many parks and zoos. Many people will _____ 14 a long way and stand in a long _____ 15 to see a lion. You can also read books that people _____ 16 about lions. You can learn how lions live and why they are much more than big house cats.

alike
while
eyes
white
line
lion
size
miles
times
nice
drive
tiny
write
inside
mine
shine

Spelling and Writing

Word List

alike
while
eyes
white
line
lion
size
miles
times
nice
drive
tiny
write
inside
mine
shine

Write to the Point

Many wildlife parks have signs near the animals' living areas. The signs give interesting facts about the animals. Choose an animal that you like. Then make a sign telling about the animal. Try to use spelling words from this lesson.

Use the strategies on page 7 when you are not sure how to spell a word.

Proofreading

Proofread the newspaper article below. Use proofreading marks to correct five spelling mistakes, three capitalization mistakes, and two punctuation mistakes.

Proofreading Marks
◯ spell correctly
≡ capitalize
⊙ add period

Lion Land Big Treat

Lion Land opened over the weekend to wild cheers People came from mils away. they stood in linne for hours to become part of this wildlife adventure. once they got insid, they could not believe their eyez. Lions strolled freely and came right up to the cars. We got just a tiney bit nervous when a lion the size of a horse looked at us through our car window. check out Lion Land for yourself. You won't be disappointed

Dictionary Skills

Guide Words   Each page in a dictionary has two words at the top. These words are called guide words. The first guide word is the first entry word on the page. The other guide word is the last entry word on the page. Guide words help you find entry words.

Look at the dictionary page below and find the guide words.

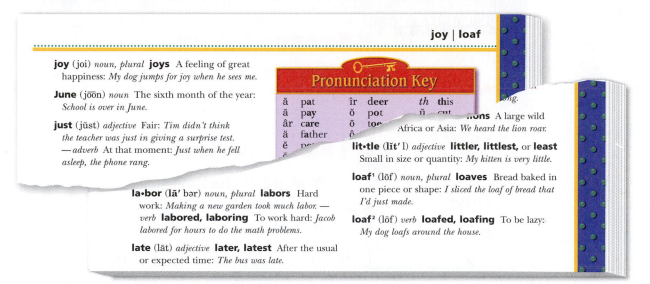

Look up these spelling words in the Spelling Dictionary. Write the guide words and page number for each.

	Guide Words		Page
1. while	_____	_____	_____
2. drive	_____	_____	_____
3. nice	_____	_____	_____
4. size	_____	_____	_____

Challenge Yourself

Use the Spelling Dictionary to answer these questions. Then use separate paper to write sentences showing that you understand the meaning of each Challenge Word.

Challenge Words

variety	admire
chime	define

5. Would you find a **variety** of toys in a toy store?   _____

6. Would most people **admire** a mud puddle?   _____

7. Do police cars and fire trucks have sirens that **chime**?   _____

8. Does a dictionary **define** words?   _____

More Words with Long *i*

night

Say and Listen

Say each spelling word. Listen for the long *i* sound.

Think and Sort

Look at the letters in each word. Think about how long *i* is spelled. Spell each word aloud.

Long *i* can be shown as /ī/. How many spelling patterns for /ī/ do you see?

1. Write the **five** spelling words that have the *i* pattern.

2. Write the **six** spelling words that have the *y* pattern.

3. Look at the word *high*. The spelling pattern for this word is *igh*. Write the **four** spelling words that have the *igh* pattern.

4. Write the **one** spelling word that has the *uy* pattern.

Use the steps on page 6 to study words that are hard for you.

Spelling list:

buy
Friday
fly
kind
why
child
mind
try
behind
sky
cry
high
right
by
light
night

1. *i* Words

_____
_____
_____
_____
_____

2. *y* Words

_____
_____
_____
_____
_____
_____

3. *igh* Words

_____
_____
_____
_____

4. *uy* Word

_____

Spelling Patterns

i	y	igh	uy
k**i**nd	tr**y**	h**igh**	b**uy**

Spelling and Meaning

Definitions Write the spelling word for each definition. Use the Spelling Dictionary if you need to.

1. at the back of   _____
2. to move through the air   _____
3. day before Saturday   _____
4. helpful   _____
5. next to   _____

Rhymes Write the spelling word that completes each sentence and rhymes with the underlined word.

6. My _____ shoe feels too <u>tight</u>.
7. The big box of toys was <u>quite</u> _____.
8. The <u>spy</u> climbed _____ in the tree.
9. The young _____ chose a book about <u>wild</u> animals.
10. Wet or <u>dry</u>, these onions make me _____.
11. Turn on the <u>light</u> to see at _____.
12. Here's a fork so you can _____ my apple <u>pie</u>.
13. What should I _____ <u>my</u> mom for her birthday?
14. Do you _____ if I close the <u>blind</u>?
15. Tell me _____ you used purple <u>dye</u>.

Word Story   One spelling word comes from the Old English word *sceo*. *Sceo* meant "cloud." The spelling word names the place where we see clouds. Write the word.

16. _____

Family Tree: *light*   Think about how the *light* words are alike in spelling and meaning. Then add another *light* word to the tree.

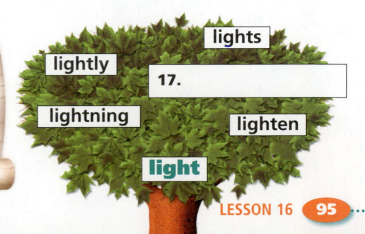

lights

lightly

17.

lightning

lighten

light

Living Room Circus

My family and I had planned to go to the

circus last _____. It was a beautiful day. The sun
                    1

was bright, and the _____ was blue. But I got sick.
                           2

Mom made a bed for me on the couch. Then she opened the

front door to let Tinker in. Tinker is our gray tabby cat. He sleeps

all day in the warm _____ of the sun. He plays all
                           3

_____. I _____ to talk Mom and Dad into
        4   5

letting me stay up all night, too. If the cat can, _____
                                                              6

can't I? They don't agree.

Well, that day Tinker dropped a fat pigeon _____
                                                    7

my dad's feet.

"Oh, no!" Mom cried. "Tinker, how could you bring that in the

house? What were you thinking?"

Mom thinks she can talk to Tinker just as she can talk to a

_____. She gets very angry when Tinker acts like a cat.
        8

Just then, the pigeon fluttered its wings. It wasn't hurt.

It began to _____ around the room.
9

Tinker saw the pigeon and hid _____ the
10

couch. He jumped out as the pigeon whizzed by.

Mom opened the door. Tinker chased the pigeon. Dad

chased Tinker. My baby brother began to _____.
11

And I began to laugh. You couldn't _____ a
12

ticket to a better show.

At last the pigeon flew out the door. Tinker was

_____ behind it. But the pigeon got away.
13

It flew _____ into the sky.
14

I was really glad that the pigeon was safe. And I didn't

_____ that I was sick. I got to see a circus after
15

all! It just wasn't the _____ of circus I expected
16

to see!

Spelling and Writing

buy
Friday
fly
kind
why
child
mind
try
behind
sky
cry
high
right
by
light
night

Write to the Point

In the story "Living Room Circus," the word *circus* means "an exciting time." Write a paragraph about an exciting time. The paragraph can be about you or someone else. Use spelling words from this lesson in your paragraph.

Use the strategies on page 7 when you are not sure how to spell a word.

Proofreading

Proofread the e-mail message below. Use proofreading marks to correct five spelling mistakes, three capitalization mistakes, and two punctuation mistakes.

Proofreading Marks
◯ spell correctly
≡ capitalize
⊙ add period

e-mail

| Address Book | Attachment | Check Spelling | Send | Save Draft | Cancel |

sam,

Tinker is in trouble again On Frieday he put my hat behinde the couch. That nighte he hid my sock He really has a miend of his own. that is whiy I love him so much.

Are you going to the cat show on Saturday? write me back and let me know. Here is a new picture of Tinker.

Betsy

Tinker

Dictionary Skills

Alphabetical Order   Many words begin with the same letter. To arrange these words in alphabetical order, look at the second letter of each word. Look at the two words below. Then complete the sentences that follow.

| sky   story |

1. *Sky* and *story* both start with the letter *s*. To put them in alphabetical order, look at the _____ letter.

2. The second letter in <u>sk</u>y is _____.

3. The second letter in <u>st</u>ory is _____.

4. In the alphabet, *k* comes before *t*, so the word _____ comes before the word _____.

In each list below, the words begin with the same letter. Look at the second letter of each word. Then write the words in alphabetical order.

5. buy   behind   by

_____

_____

_____

6. fly   Friday   finish

_____

_____

_____

Challenge Yourself

Write the Challenge Word for each clue. Check the Spelling Dictionary to see if you are right. Then use separate paper to write sentences showing that you understand the meaning of each Challenge Word.

Challenge Words

designer   glider
cycle   skyline

7. It has big wings but is not a bird.   _____

8. A big city has one of these.   _____

9. If you ride something with wheels, you may have this.

_____

10. This is a person who makes drawings and plans.   _____

Lesson 17
Words with -ed or -ing

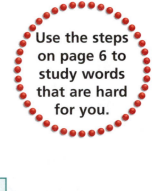
laughing

1. -ed Words

_____
_____
_____
_____
_____
_____
_____
_____
_____

2. -ing Words

_____
_____
_____
_____
_____
_____

ending
wished
asked
guessing
laughing
dreamed
rained
meeting
sleeping
handed
painted
filled
reading
subtracted
thanked
waited

Say and Listen

Say the spelling words. Listen for the -ed and -ing endings.

Think and Sort

Each spelling word is formed by adding -ed or -ing to a base word. A **base word** is a word from which other words are formed. The base word for _wished_ is _wish_. The base word for _ending_ is _end_.

Look at each spelling word. Think about the base word and the ending. Spell each word aloud.

1. Write the **ten** spelling words that end in -ed.

2. Write the **six** spelling words that end in -ing.

Use the steps on page 6 to study words that are hard for you.

Spelling Patterns

-ed	-ing
paint**ed**	read**ing**

Spelling and Meaning

Definitions   Write the spelling word for each definition.
Use the Spelling Dictionary if you need to.

1. passed with one's hands _____

2. said that one was pleased _____

3. stayed _____

4. a coming together for some purpose _____

5. forming an opinion without all the facts _____

6. saw or thought during sleep _____

7. fell in drops of water from the clouds _____

Analogies   Write the spelling word that completes each analogy.

8. *Taught* is to *instructed* as *hoped* is to _____.

9. *Dress* is to *sewed* as *picture* is to _____.

10. *Playing* is to *piano* as _____ is to *book*.

11. *Chair* is to *sitting* as *bed* is to _____.

12. *Told* is to *explained* as *questioned* is to _____.

13. *Happy* is to _____ as *sad* is to *crying*.

14. *Beginning* is to *start* as _____ is to *finish*.

15. *Out* is to *emptied* as *in* is to _____.

Word Story   One of the spelling words comes from two Latin words—*sub* and *trahere*. *Sub* meant "below or away." *Trahere* meant "to pull." *Subtrahere* meant "to pull away." Write the spelling word that comes from *subtrahere*.

16. _____

Family Tree: *rained*   *Rained* is a form of *rain*. Think about how the *rain* words are alike in spelling and meaning. Then add another *rain* word to the tree.

- raining
- rains
- 17.
- rainier
- rainless
- rainy
- **rain**

The Playoffs

When I left hockey practice yesterday, it was still raining. It had

_____ all day. I _____ for Dad to pick me up.
　　　　1　　　　　　　　　　　　　　　　2

Then I remembered that Mom and Dad were _____ with
　　　　　　　　　　　　　　　　　　　　　　3

teachers and other parents. They were planning our fall festival, so I walked

over to school to wait.

I tried not to think about the homework that I hadn't done yet.

I had extra math problems to do because I added numbers on our last

test when I should have _____ them. Oh, how I
　　　　　　　　　　　　　4

_____ that I had done my homework before practice.
　　　5

Then I would have been finished.

At school I ran into Ms. Ford, the art teacher. She was showing the

parents some pictures that students had _____. Mr. Chan,
　　　　　　　　　　　　　　　　　　　　　6

the librarian, was also at school. I _____ him if I could wait
　　　　　　　　　　　　　　　　　7

in the library. He said yes.

I started doing my math homework. It was going pretty well. Then

Mr. Chan _____ me a book that he was sure I would like. I
　　　　　　8

_____ him and looked at the cover.
　　9

The book was about my favorite hockey player, Wayne Gretzky. It was

_____ with pictures of him. I started _____.
　　　10　　　　　　　　　　　　　　　　　　　　　11

The book was great. It started with his childhood. I could hardly wait to

read the _____.
　　　　　12

The next thing I knew, I was on the floor, swinging my arms and yelling. Mom and Dad were there in the library. They were

_____ at me. I shook my head and blinked.
13

"Was I _____?" I asked.
14

"I'm only _____," Dad said, "but I would
15

say you _____ you were a hockey player.
16

The way you were swinging your arms around, I'm glad I wasn't on the other team!"

I grinned. Too bad it was just a dream.

ending
wished
asked
guessing
laughing
dreamed
rained
meeting
sleeping
handed
painted
filled
reading
subtracted
thanked
waited

Word List

ending
wished
asked
guessing
laughing
dreamed
rained
meeting
sleeping
handed
painted
filled
reading
subtracted
thanked
waited

Write to the Point

You dream almost every time you sleep. Dreams can take you on great adventures. Sometimes dreams are happy. Other times they're silly. Write a paragraph about a dream you've had. Try to use spelling words from this lesson.

Use the strategies on page 7 when you are not sure how to spell a word.

Proofreading

Proofread the movie review below. Use proofreading marks to correct five spelling mistakes, three capitalization mistakes, and two unnecessary words.

Proofreading Marks
◯ spell correctly
≡ capitalize
℘ take out

The Winning Team ★★★★

Is a Winner!

this movie is about a losing hockey team. The

coach has tried everything to to help the team win.

he called a meating each day before practice. He

thankt the players for their hard work but told them

he wisht they would do better. He askt the players to

run five miles a day, even when it it rained. the

surprise endin shows what really worked.

Language Connection

End Punctuation Use a period at the end of a sentence that tells or explains something. Use a question mark at the end of a sentence that asks a question. Use an exclamation point at the end of a sentence that shows strong feeling or surprise. In sentences that have quotation marks, place the end punctuation inside the quotation marks.

> Matt said, "Here comes the team**.**"

> The police officer yelled, "Open that door!"

Write the following sentences, using periods, question marks, and exclamation points correctly.

1. Betsy asked Paul, "Who painted this picture"

   _____

2. She saw that Paul was sleeping

   _____

3. Betsy shouted, "Boo"

   _____

4. Paul jumped up fast

   _____

5. "Oh, Betsy," he cried. "Now I'll never know the ending of my dream"

   _____

6. They both started laughing

   _____

Challenge Yourself

What do you think each Challenge Word means? Check the Spelling Dictionary to see if you are right. Then use separate paper to write sentences showing that you understand the meaning of each Challenge Word.

Challenge Words
fulfilling
faltering
consented
governed

7. He is **fulfilling** his promise.

8. A beginning skater may make **faltering** movements on the ice.

9. Mom **consented** to let us play.

10. The President **governed** the country for four years.

Lesson 18

Unit 3 Review
Lessons 13–17

Use the steps on page 6 to study words that are hard for you.

13

butter
hundred
done
lovely
won

More Words with Short *u*

Write the spelling word for each clue.

1. People often use this word to describe flowers. _____

2. This is the sum of 99 and 1. _____

3. If you came in first, you did this. _____

4. You can spread this on bread. _____

5. When you are finished, you are this. _____

14

which
children
pretty
build
been

Words with Short *i*

Write the spelling word that belongs in each group.

6. where   when _____
7. be   being _____
8. beautiful   lovely _____
9. form   make _____
10. tots   youngsters _____

15

while
write
tiny
lion
eyes

Words with Long *i*

Write the spelling word for each definition.

11. the body parts used for seeing _____
12. to make letters on a surface _____
13. a large wild cat _____

14. although   _____

15. very small   _____

16

behind
why
right
night
buy

More Words with Long *i*

Write the spelling word that has the same meaning as the word or words in dark type.

16. **For what reason** did the pioneers go west?

_____

17. Can I **pay for** this toy?

_____

18. You were **correct** about the weather.   _____

19. Last **evening** I had a strange dream.

_____

20. Please stand **in back of** me in line.

_____

17

wished
thanked
dreamed
guessing
laughing

Words with *-ed* or *-ing*

Write the spelling word that completes each sentence.

21. They are _____ at your joke.

22. Alicia _____ for a new bicycle.

23. Are you just _____ the answer?

24. Amad _____ about winning a trophy.

25. The teacher _____ the children for the gift.

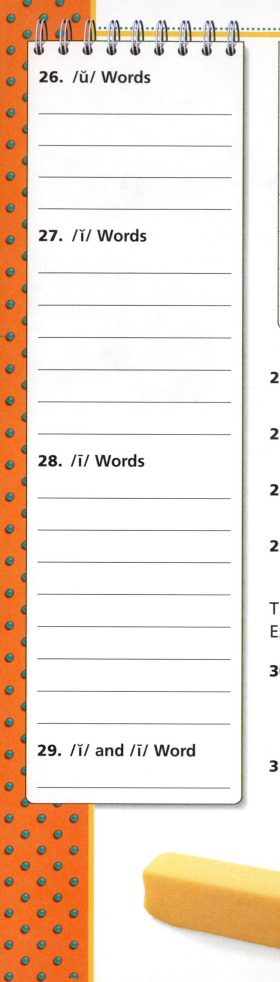

26. /ŭ/ Words

_____
_____
_____

27. /ĭ/ Words

_____
_____
_____
_____
_____
_____

28. /ī/ Words

_____
_____
_____
_____
_____
_____
_____
_____

29. /ĭ/ and /ī/ Word

_____

Review Sort

children	won	behind	right
been	write	lovely	why
done	eyes	which	while
night	buy	butter	wished
tiny	pretty	build	

26. Write the **four** short *u* words. Circle the letter or letters that spell /ŭ/ in each word.

27. Write the **six** short *i* words. Circle the letter or letters that spell /ĭ/ in each word.

28. Write the **eight** long *i* words. Circle the letter or letters that spell /ī/ in each word.

29. Write the **one** word that has both short *i* and long *i*.

These five words have been sorted into two groups. Explain how the words in each group are alike.

30.   wished   thanked   dreamed

_____
_____

31.   laughing   guessing

_____
_____

Writer's Workshop

A Friendly Letter

Everyone likes to get letters from friends and family members. People write friendly letters to tell about themselves, their thoughts, and their feelings. Here are the greeting and body of Amber's letter to her friend Chelsey.

110 Winn Drive
Smithville, AZ
December 5, 2003

Dear Chelsey,

Our new house is great! I can see the park from my bedroom window. Sometimes I walk there with Theo. He loves to chase the birds. When they fly away, he barks and runs in circles.

A nice girl named Keisha lives next door.

Prewriting   To write her letter, Amber followed the steps in the writing process. After she decided to whom she should write, she made a list. The list helped her decide what to tell Chelsey. Part of Amber's list is shown here. Study what she did.

New House
can see park
Theo chases birds
park closed Monday

New Friend
Keisha

It's Your Turn!

Write your own friendly letter. Tell about something that happened or about your thoughts and feelings. After you have decided whom you will write, make a list of the things you want to say. Then follow the other steps in the writing process—writing, revising, proofreading, and publishing. Try to use spelling words from this lesson in your letter.

Words with Short o

clock

1. o Words

_____
_____
_____
_____
_____
_____
_____
_____
_____
_____
_____
_____
_____

2. a Words

_____
_____
_____

October
shop
block
bottle
o'clock
sorry
socks
problem
what
jog
wash
was
clock
bottom
forgot
body

Say and Listen

Say each spelling word. Listen for the short o sound.

Think and Sort

Look at the letters in each word. Think about how short o is spelled. Spell each word aloud.

Short o can be shown as /ŏ/. How many spelling patterns for /ŏ/ do you see?

1. Write the **thirteen** spelling words that have the _o_ pattern.

2. Write the **three** spelling words that have the _a_ pattern.

Use the steps on page 6 to study words that are hard for you.

Spelling Patterns

o	a
sh**o**p	w**a**s

Spelling and Meaning

Clues Write the spelling word for each clue.

1. clothes that belong on your feet _____
2. has streets on all sides _____
3. in a group with *walk* and *run* _____
4. feeling regret _____
5. a question word _____
6. opposite of *remembered* _____
7. means "of the clock" _____

Analogies Write the spelling word that completes each analogy.

8. *Have* is to *has* as *were* is to _____.
9. *Month* is to _____ as *day* is to *Monday*.
10. *Bark* is to *tree* as *skin* is to _____.
11. *Top* is to _____ as *up* is to *down*.
12. *Learn* is to *school* as _____ is to *store*.
13. *Solution* is to _____ as *answer* is to *question*.
14. *Soap* is to _____ as *towel* is to *dry*.
15. *Catsup* is to _____ as *pickle* is to *jar*.

Word Story One of the spelling words names an instrument for telling time. Many years ago, the instrument contained bells to sound out passing hours. The word comes from the Latin word *clocca*, which meant "bells." Write the word.

16. _____

Family Tree: *wash* Think about how the *wash* words are alike in spelling and meaning. Then add another *wash* word to the tree.

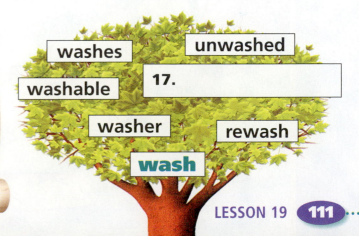

washes

unwashed

washable

17.

washer

rewash

wash

Use each spelling word once to complete the story.

The Problem with P.J.

The _____ with P.J. was that she read too many
mystery books. In September she read 15 mysteries. So far in the
month of _____, she had read 12.

P.J. had told Sonya all about every one of the books. Sonya
_____ tired of hearing about P.J.'s mysteries. She
decided to let P.J. know.

One afternoon when the hall
_____ struck four, P.J.
started out on her daily two-mile
_____. She went around
the _____ and into the
center of town. Then she jogged past the
candy _____ and headed
down to the lake.

As she ran by the lake, something caught her eye. It looked like a _____ 8 floating in the lake. She could see something white at the _____ 9 of the bottle. It looked like a rolled-up piece of paper. She could hardly believe it. Here was her chance to solve a real mystery!

It was getting late. P.J. knew that she had to be home by five _____ 10. She was in such a hurry to get the bottle that she _____ 11 to be careful. SPLASH! P.J.'s _____ 12 was soaked from head to toe. But she had the bottle. She wondered _____ 13 the message said. Quickly P.J. opened the bottle. She shook out the piece of paper and began to read.

"I am _____ 14 you had to go through all this. I'll bet your shoes and _____ 15 are soaking wet. I hope the water will _____ 16 away your taste for mysteries. Guess who."

Suddenly P.J. heard a giggle. She knew that laugh anywhere! P.J. ran over to the big oak tree. Sonya jumped out from behind it, and both girls laughed. This mystery had been solved!

October
shop
block
bottle
o'clock
sorry
socks
problem
what
jog
wash
was
clock
bottom
forgot
body

Spelling and Writing

October
shop
block
bottle
o'clock
sorry
socks
problem
what
jog
wash
was
clock
bottom
forgot
body

Write to the Point

Have you ever had a problem with a friend? Perhaps you had trouble agreeing about something. What did you do to make things better? Write a paragraph that tells the problem and what you did to solve it. Use spelling words from this lesson in your paragraph.

Use the strategies on page 7 when you are not sure how to spell a word.

Proofreading

Proofread the journal entry below. Use proofreading marks to correct five spelling mistakes, three capitalization mistakes, and two punctuation mistakes.

Proofreading Marks
◯ spell correctly
≡ capitalize
⊙ add period

October 18

today I have a mystery to solve. My running sox and hat were at the botom of the stairs when I got home from school Now it is time for my jogg around the blak, but there is a problum. they are both missing. Mom says she didn't move them Nobody is here but Mom and me. Maybe sparky has moved them. I haven't seen that dog since four o'clock.

Dictionary Skills

Alphabetical Order   The words *block, bottle,* and *butter* begin with the same letter, *b*. To arrange words that begin with the same letter in alphabetical order, use the second letter.

| **b**lock   **bo**ttle   **bu**tter |

Write each group of words in alphabetical order.

1. cover   clock   cap   children

_____

_____

_____

_____

2. shop   salt   sorry   stack

_____

_____

_____

_____

3. wash   wonder   west   what

_____

_____

_____

_____

4. forgot   feed   funny   farmer

_____

_____

_____

_____

Challenge Yourself

What do you think each Challenge Word means? Check the Spelling Dictionary to see if you are right. Then use separate paper to write sentences showing that you understand the meaning of each Challenge Word.

Challenge Words

deposit   apologize
waffle   comment

5. Marie decided to **deposit** a note in the bottle.

6. You should **apologize** when you hurt someone's feelings.

7. A hot **waffle** would taste good for breakfast.

8. What **comment** did his father make about Chen's grades?

Words with Long *o*

1. o-consonant-e Words

_____
_____
_____
_____
_____
_____
_____

2. ow Words

_____
_____
_____
_____
_____
_____

3. oe Words

_____
_____

4. o Word

_____

slow
whole
hope
blow
joke
wrote
show
yellow
goes
toe
alone
hole
snow
close
November
know

Say and Listen

Say each spelling word. Listen for the long *o* sound.

Think and Sort

Look at the letters in each word. Think about how long *o* is spelled. Spell each word aloud.

Long *o* can be shown as /ō/. How many spelling patterns for /ō/ do you see?

1. Write the **seven** spelling words that have the *o-consonant-e* pattern.

2. Write the **six** spelling words that have the *ow* pattern.

3. Write the **two** spelling words that have the *oe* pattern.

4. Write the **one** spelling word that has the *o* pattern.

Use the steps on page 6 to study words that are hard for you.

Spelling Patterns

o-consonant-e	ow	oe	o
hope	slow	toe	November

Spelling and Meaning

Definitions   Write the spelling word for each definition.
Use the Spelling Dictionary if you need to.

1. moves; travels   _____

2. made words with a pen   _____

3. to wish for something   _____

4. the entire amount   _____

5. to be familiar with   _____

6. by oneself   _____

Analogies   Write the spelling word that completes each analogy.

7. *Shape* is to *square* as *color* is to _____.

8. *Lose* is to *win* as _____ is to *open*.

9. *January* is to *February* as _____ is to *December.*

10. *Hand* is to *finger* as *foot* is to _____.

11. *Hot* is to *fire* as *cold* is to _____.

12. *Beat* is to *drum* as _____ is to *whistle.*

13. *Write* is to *letter* as *dig* is to _____.

14. *Rabbit* is to *fast* as *tortoise* is to _____.

15. *Day* is to *night* as _____ is to *hide*.

Word Story   Long ago Latin had the word *jocus.* The French changed the word to *jogleor,* which meant "juggler." A juggler does funny things. Later the English changed *jocus* to a word that means "something funny." Write the word.

16. _____

Family Tree: *know*   Think about how the *know* words are alike in spelling and meaning. Then add another *know* word to the tree.

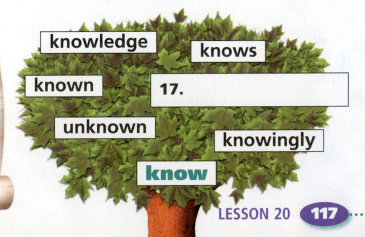

knowledge
knows
known
17.
unknown
knowingly
know

Use each spelling word once to complete the story.

What Are Friends For?

Jacob wanted to go to Salvador's house on Saturday. Salvador _____ a note to
1

Jacob. Salvador said he wanted to be _____. Jacob
2

knew Salvador was sad because his dog had run away. Jacob decided to go to Salvador's house anyway.

Jacob had a plan. He would tell _____ after joke.
3

He would make Salvador laugh if it took the _____ day
4

to do it.

"Why did the boy _____ the door and leave his
5

father outside in the month of _____?" Jacob asked.
6

Salvador didn't answer. He stared at his dog's picture.

"Because he wanted a cold pop." Jacob laughed. Salvador didn't even smile.

Jacob asked, "What kind of nail hurts when you hit it?" Salvador didn't look up.

"A _____ nail." Jacob
7

smiled. Salvador didn't.

Jacob tried again. "What comes after a snowstorm?" Salvador didn't answer.

Jacob said, "_____
8

shovels. Here is another one. What

_____ away when you fill it up?"
9

"I wish you would go away," Salvador said.

Jacob was hurt. He tried not to _____
10
it. He knew Salvador was hurting, too. Jacob said, "A

_____. What did the north wind say to the
11

west wind?"

"I don't _____," answered Salvador.
12

Jacob told him anyway. "It's time to _____."
13

"I _____ you don't have any more awful
14

jokes," Salvador said.

Jacob gave up. He ran out the door. Salvador yelled,

"Jacob, _____ down!"
15

Jacob tripped on the steps. He flew up in the air and

landed in a pile of bright red and _____ leaves.
16

All Salvador could see was Jacob's nose. Salvador laughed

and laughed.

Salvador wiped his eyes and said, "Thanks for cheering

me up."

Jacob smiled and said, "That's what friends are

for, Salvador!"

slow
whole
hope
blow
joke
wrote
show
yellow
goes
toe
alone
hole
snow
close
November
know

slow
whole
hope
blow
joke
wrote
show
yellow
goes
toe
alone
hole
snow
close
November
know

Write to the Point

Jacob told Salvador jokes to make him laugh. They didn't work. Write a joke or riddle that makes you laugh. You may write one that you have heard before. You can also make up a new one of your own. Try to use spelling words from this lesson in your joke or riddle.

Use the strategies on page 7 when you are not sure how to spell a word.

Proofreading

Proofread the letter below. Use proofreading marks to correct five spelling mistakes, three capitalization mistakes, and two punctuation mistakes.

Proofreading Marks
◯ spell correctly
≡ capitalize
⊙ add period

214 Spring Street

Flint Hill, VA 22627

November 29, 2003

Dear Joe,

I kno I haven't written lately. i hoppe you

are not mad. thanks for the yello sweater It

gose great with my blue jacket.

Here's a good joke. why did the pill wear a

blanket? It was a cold tablet

Moe

Joe Jones
54321 Lone Oak Road
Soapstone Falls, OH 65432

Language Connection

Verbs   Action words are called verbs. The spelling words in the boxes are verbs.

Unscramble the letters of the spelling words in the sentences below. Write each sentence and then circle the verb.

wrote

goes

know

1. Jack hurt his oet.

_____

2. Please wosh me your new shoes.

_____

3. nows fell all night long.

_____

4. We ate the lewoh pizza.

_____

5. Krista bought a loweyl skateboard.

_____

6. Scooter dug a lohe in the yard.

_____

7. Ming twore a story about a crow.

_____

8. Mrs. Sosa egos to lunch with our class.

_____

Challenge Yourself

Write the Challenge Word for each clue. Check the Spelling Dictionary to see if you are right. Then use separate paper to write sentences showing that you understand the meaning of each Challenge Word.

Challenge Words

console	dome
adobe	rodent

9. The roof of some buildings is one of these. _____

10. A mouse is this kind of animal. _____

11. Some homes in the Southwest are made of this. _____

12. You might do this to a friend who is sad. _____

More Words with Long *o*

cocoa

1. *o* Words

_____
_____
_____
_____
_____
_____
_____
_____
_____
_____

2. *oa* Words

_____
_____
_____
_____
_____

3. *o* and *oa* Word

_____

most
coat
ago
hold
hello
cocoa
open
loaf
over
comb
toast
almost
boat
both
road
gold

Say and Listen

Say each spelling word. Listen for the long *o* sound.

Think and Sort

Look at the letters in each word. Think about how long *o* is spelled. Spell each word aloud.

Long *o* can be shown as /ō/. How many spelling patterns for /ō/ do you see?

1. Write the **ten** spelling words that have the *o* pattern.

2. Write the **five** spelling words that have the *oa* pattern.

3. Write the **one** spelling word that has both the *o* and *oa* patterns.

Use the steps on page 6 to study words that are hard for you.

Spelling Patterns

o	oa
m**o**st	b**oa**t

Spelling and Meaning

Definitions   Write the spelling word for each definition.
Use the Spelling Dictionary if you need to.

1. to arrange the hair   _____

2. a precious metal   _____

3. in the past   _____

4. the one as well as the other   _____

5. a greeting   _____

6. to keep in the hand   _____

7. the greatest amount   _____

8. nearly   _____

9. to cause something to be no longer closed _____

10. above   _____

11. bread baked in one piece   _____

Classifying   Write the spelling word that belongs in each group.

12. hat   scarf   gloves   _____

13. milk   eggs   cereal   _____

14. street   avenue   lane   _____

15. car   train   airplane   _____

Word Story   One of the spelling words was once spelled *cacao,* but many people misspelled it. They confused the word with *coco,* the name of the tree on which coconuts grow. Write the spelling word as it is spelled today.

16. _____

Family Tree: *toast*   Think about how the *toast* words are alike in spelling and meaning. Then add another *toast* word to the tree.

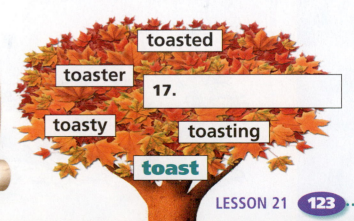

toasted

toaster

17.

toasty   toasting

toast

Use each spelling word once to complete the story.

Gold Island

We spent last week at a lake that had an island in the middle of it. The island was tiny. It was called Gold Island. A legend says that a treasure was buried there many years _____. The treasure was never found.

     ₁

My sister, Jasmine, was excited about the legend. One day she packed a _____ of bread and some cheese. Then she got

     ₂

into a small _____ and rowed to the island. Jasmine

     ₃

was going to search every inch of it until she found the treasure.

Jasmine had been gone _____ three hours when a

     ₄

storm came up. _____ Mom and Dad were worried. So

     ₅

was I. Jasmine can take care of herself _____ of the

     ₆

time. But this was the worst storm I had ever seen.

Just then, Jasmine came running down the _____

     ₇

to our cabin. "_____!" she yelled as she came inside,

     ₈

dripping water all _____ everything.

     ₉

"You need to change those wet clothes and _____

     ₁₀

your hair," Dad said.

I said I would make some _____ and
                              11
_____.
        12

"Wait," said Jasmine. "The storm blew over a tree on the island. I found something interesting buried under it." She reached into her _____ pockets. "Please close
                              13
your eyes and then _____ out your hands." We
                          14
thought she was crazy. But we did it. Jasmine put rocks into our hands.

"Okay," she said, "_____ your eyes."
                          15
The rocks looked just like _____. Then Mom
                              16
said, "Now I know why you are so excited. I hate to spoil your fun. These rocks only *look* like gold."

"It's easy to be fooled," Dad said. "That's why people call them fool's gold."

Jasmine hadn't found a treasure after all. But now we know another reason why the island is called Gold Island.

most
coat
ago
hold
hello
cocoa
open
loaf
over
comb
toast
almost
boat
both
road
gold

Spelling and Writing

most
coat
ago
hold
hello
cocoa
open
loaf
over
comb
toast
almost
boat
both
road
gold

Write to the Point

Jasmine was excited by the legend of the buried treasure. Write a paragraph about a buried treasure you would like to find. What is the treasure? Where will you find it? Try to use spelling words from the lesson.

Use the strategies on page 7 when you are not sure how to spell a word.

Proofreading

Proofread the e-mail below. Use proofreading marks to correct five spelling mistakes, three capitalization mistakes, and two punctuation mistakes.

Proofreading Marks
◯ spell correctly
≡ capitalize
? add question mark

e-mail

| Address Book | Attachment | Check Spelling | Send | Save Draft | Cancel |

Helo, adam. We went to a lake last week. It had an island in the middle. I thought I had found some goold, but it was only rocks. Are you ready for our trip to the beach We'll combe the beach for seashells early in the morning. we can eat breakfast before we go. Mom baked a lofe of bread. do you like toest with jam

Jasmine

Language Connection

Synonyms   Synonyms are words that have the same meaning. The words *hello, howdy,* and *hi* are synonyms.

Use spelling words from this lesson to write synonym clues for the puzzle.

ACROSS

3. _____

4. _____

6. _____

7. _____

DOWN

1. _____

2. _____

3. _____

5. _____

6. _____

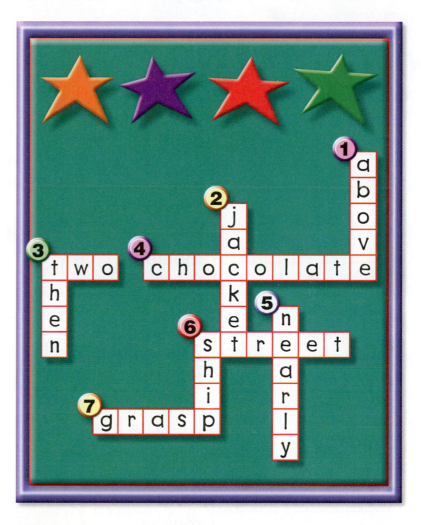

Challenge Yourself

Use the Spelling Dictionary to answer these questions. Then use separate paper to write sentences showing that you understand the meaning of each Challenge Word.

Challenge Words	
coax	solo
rodeo	patrol

8. Would a person **coax** cereal into a bowl?   _____

9. Could one person go on a **solo** bicycle ride?   _____

10. Would you find a **rodeo** in the middle of a lake?   _____

11. Do police officers go on **patrol**?   _____

Lesson 22

Words with /o͝o/

cook

1. oo Words

_____
_____
_____
_____
_____
_____
_____
_____
_____

2. u, u-consonant-e Words

_____
_____
_____
_____

3. ou Words

_____
_____
_____

book
took
cook
sure
should
stood
wood
put
poor
foot
shook
would
full
cookies
pull
could

Say and Listen

Say each spelling word. Listen for the vowel sound you hear in *book*.

Think and Sort

Look at the letters in each word. Think about how the vowel sound in *book* is spelled. Spell each word aloud.

The vowel sound in *book* can be shown as /o͝o/. How many spelling patterns for /o͝o/ do you see?

1. Write the **nine** spelling words that have the *oo* pattern.

2. Write the **four** spelling words that have the *u* or *u*-consonant-*e* pattern.

3. Write the **three** spelling words that have the *ou* pattern.

Use the steps on page 6 to study words that are hard for you.

Spelling Patterns

oo	u	u-consonant-e	ou
b**oo**k	p**u**t	s**u**re	w**ou**ld

Spelling and Meaning

Antonyms   Write the spelling word that is an antonym of each word.

1. push   _____
2. sat   _____
3. uncertain   _____
4. rich   _____
5. empty   _____
6. gave   _____

Clues   Write the spelling word for each clue.

7. You put a shoe on this part of your body.   _____
8. This word means "ought to."   _____
9. Logs are made of this.   _____
10. Most people like these sweet treats.   _____
11. This word means "was able to."   _____
12. You might do this to prepare food.   _____
13. This word means "to set."   _____
14. This word sounds like *wood*.   _____
15. This word is the past tense of *shake*.   _____

Word Story   Many years ago in England, people used the wood from beech trees to write on. One spelling word comes from *boece*, which meant "beech." Write the word.

16. _____

Family Tree: cook   Think about how the *cook* words are alike in spelling and meaning. Then add another *cook* word to the tree.

cooker   cookies

cooking   17.

cooked   uncooked

cook

The Little Mouse

Marvin the mouse peeked over

a big pile of _____.
            1
The lion was asleep. Then

Marvin's whiskers twitched.

He smelled the chocolate

_____ lying beside the lion's _____.
          2   3
Marvin wondered if he _____ try to get one of the
                              4
cookies. The little mouse was very hungry. He decided to take

the chance.

Marvin tiptoed over to the lion. He slowly reached out to

_____ the cookies toward him.
        5
Whack! The lion _____ his big foot down on the
                        6
little mouse. Then the lion _____ up and roared.
                                  7
Marvin was scared. He _____ like a leaf.
                            8
Marvin was afraid, but he was also smart. He did some fast

thinking. He said, "Mr. Lion, I'm just a _____ little
                                              9
mouse. You would have to build a fire to _____ me.
                                                10
Are you really _____ I would be worth the trouble?"
                      11
The lion thought about it. He was still very _____
                                                    12
from his last meal. The lion told Marvin to hurry away before he

changed his mind. Marvin thanked him and was gone.

The next day two hunters were looking for big game. They had read in a _____ that there were lots
13
of lions nearby. The hunters saw the sleeping lion. They _____ out a net and threw it over him.
14
There was nothing the lion _____ do except
15
yell for help.

Marvin heard the lion's cry. He looked until he found the lion. He said he _____ try to help. The
16
lion said, "You are too small to help."

Marvin didn't answer. He began to nibble on the net with his sharp teeth. Soon the little mouse had made a big hole. The lion slipped out of the net. He was free!

That is how the lion learned that good things often come in small packages.

book
took
cook
sure
should
stood
wood
put
poor
foot
shook
would
full
cookies
pull
could

Spelling and Writing

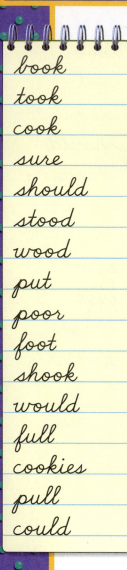

book
took
cook
sure
should
stood
wood
put
poor
foot
shook
would
full
cookies
pull
could

Write to the Point

A lion with good manners would thank the mouse for saving his life. Write a thank-you note to a person who has helped you. Include what the person did and why you are happy the person helped you. Try to use spelling words from this lesson in your thank-you note.

Use the strategies on page 7 when you are not sure how to spell a word.

Proofreading

Proofread the story review below. Use proofreading marks to correct five spelling mistakes, three capitalization mistakes, and two unnecessary words.

Proofreading Marks
◯ spell correctly
≡ capitalize
℘ take out

Story Review

The Lion and the Mouse is an an old story that has stod the test of time. the beginning will pul you into the story. what will happen to that that poer little mouse? Culd the lion be kind enough to let him go? What lesson does the story teach? If you have read the story before, then you know. if not, read it soon. You are shure to enjoy it.

Language Connection

Capital Letters The names of cities and states always begin with a capital letter.

> **P**hoenix is the capital of **A**rizona.

Unscramble the spelling words in the sentences below. Then write the sentences, using capital letters correctly.

1. many dowo products come from maine.

_____

2. i am rues that the largest state is alaska.

_____

3. everyone dosluh visit chicago, illinois.

_____

4. dowlu you like to go to new orleans?

_____

5. san francisco ohsko during an earthquake.

_____

6. my friend from toronto sent me some okecois.

_____

Challenge Yourself

What do you think each Challenge Word means? Check the Spelling Dictionary to see if you are right. Then use separate paper to write sentences showing that you understand the meaning of each Challenge Word.

Challenge Words	
bureau	gourmet
assure	endure

7. A mouse was living in a drawer of my **bureau**.

8. It nibbled on the **gourmet** cheese Mom bought.

9. Can you **assure** me it has gone and won't come back?

10. I could not **endure** one more night of its noisy squeaks.

More Words with -ed or -ing

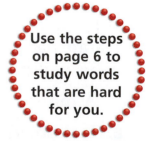

smiling

Notebook

1. Final e Dropped

_____
_____
_____
_____
_____
_____
_____
_____
_____

2. Final Consonant Doubled

_____
_____
_____
_____
_____
_____
_____

Spelling Words

sneezed
smiling
beginning
hoped
dropping
shining
stopped
pleased
dropped
liked
taking
driving
closed
jogged
hopping
shopping

Say and Listen

Say the spelling words. Listen for the -ed and -ing endings.

Think and Sort

Each spelling word is formed by adding -ed or -ing to a base word. Look at the letters in each spelling word. Spell each word aloud. Think about how the spelling of the base word changes.

1. If a base word ends in *e*, the *e* is usually dropped before -ed or -ing is added. Write the **nine** spelling words in which the final *e* of the base word is dropped.

2. If a base word ends in a single vowel and a single consonant, the consonant is often doubled before -ed or -ing is added. Write the **seven** spelling words in which the final consonant of the base word is doubled.

Use the steps on page 6 to study words that are hard for you.

Spelling Patterns

Final e Dropped	Final Consonant Doubled
take + ing = taking	begin + ing = beginning

Spelling and Meaning

Synonyms   Write the spelling word that is a synonym for each word.

1. trotted   _____
2. starting   _____
3. shut   _____
4. wished   _____
5. enjoyed   _____
6. sparkling   _____
7. quit   _____
8. grinning   _____
9. jumping   _____

Rhymes   Write the spelling word that completes each sentence and rhymes with the underlined word.

10. The singer was not <u>pleased</u> when I _____.

11. Are you _____ the cake you are <u>making</u>?

12. The bus <u>stopped</u>, and my backpack _____.

13. To turn <u>diving</u> into _____, add the letter *r*.

14. Mom was not _____ when I <u>teased</u> my brother.

15. I keep _____ the jelly and <u>mopping</u> up the mess.

Word Story   Long ago in England, people sold things in places called *schoppes*. A *schoppe* was a booth in a marketplace. Write the spelling word you can make from this word plus *-ing*.

16. _____

Family Tree: *pleased*   *Pleased* is a form of *please*. Think about how the *please* words are alike in spelling and meaning. Then add another *please* word to the tree.

pleased

pleasing

17.

pleasure   unpleasant

please

Use each spelling word once to complete the selection.

Puppy Love

Have you always _____ dogs? Have
1
you ever _____ to own one? Suppose
2
that you now have a new puppy. What do you need
to know?

At the _____ of a young puppy's life, it needs three good
3
meals a day. After it is five months old or so, your pup may need only two
meals a day. Be sure to feed your puppy only dog food. If you have been

_____ leftovers from your dinner plate into your puppy's
4
dish, you should stop. People food is not always good for
animals. Dogs need dog food. They also need lots
of water.

Handle your puppy gently. Be careful. It may
try to squirm and wiggle out of your arms. Your puppy
could get badly hurt if you _____ it.
5
Do not get in the habit of _____ your
6
pup to bed with you. A puppy can sleep in your bedroom,
but it should stay in its own bed. Also, be sure your doors
are _____. This way, your
7
puppy will not get out and hurt itself or
your things at night.

Teach your puppy good manners. It should not be jumping on everyone and _____ onto every lap. This kind of
8
behavior must be _____. Put the puppy back on the
9
floor. Say in a firm voice, "No, Scooter. No." Soon you will be
_____ at how well your puppy behaves.
10

Pay attention to your puppy's health. If your pup has coughed
or _____ for several days, take it to a vet. Even if
11
your pup is healthy, take it in for regular checkups and shots.

When your puppy is outdoors, keep it on a leash. A leash
helps keep a dog away from people, other animals, and traffic.
After you have played ball or _____ a few blocks
12
with your puppy, give it some cool water. Let it rest or nap for a
while, too.

Get your puppy used to riding in a car. Make sure it is in its
carrier while the driver is _____.
13
Also make sure someone stays with your
puppy when you or a family member is
_____ in a store. Never
14
leave your puppy alone in a closed car,
especially when it is hot and the sun is
_____. This is dangerous!
15
Taking care of a puppy is a big job.
Learn all you can about pet care. That way,
both you and your pup can keep laughing
and _____.
16

sneezed
smiling
beginning
hoped
dropping
shining
stopped
pleased
dropped
liked
taking
driving
closed
jogged
hopping
shopping

Spelling and Writing

Use the strategies on page 7 when you are not sure how to spell a word.

sneezed
smiling
beginning
hoped
dropping
shining
stopped
pleased
dropped
liked
taking
driving
closed
jogged
hopping
shopping

Write to the Point

Write a paragraph about something fun you can do with a pet. Tell where you can go and what you can do. Try to use spelling words from this lesson.

Proofreading

Proofread the letter below. Use proofreading marks to correct five spelling mistakes, three capitalization mistakes, and two punctuation mistakes.

Proofreading Marks
◯ spell correctly
≡ capitalize
⊙ add period

2616 Lakeview Drive

Gilbert, AZ 85234

May 15, 2003

Dear Tyler,

Last week we stoped by the animal shelter. i likd the kittens a lot. my parents said we could get one I was so pleaseed that I couldn't stop smilling. when we were driveing home, I thought of you. Please come see my new kitten soon

Your friend,

Samara

Language Connection

Commas To make it easy to read a date, use a comma between the day and the year.

> July 4, 1776   December 27, 1998

Decide which word from the boxes below completes each sentence. Then write the sentences, using commas correctly.

jogged **closed** **dropped** **hoped**

1. School ___ for vacation on May 28 2001.

   _____

2. On June 25 1996, Ms. Padden ___ in a race.

   _____

3. Old friends ___ in to visit us on February 4 2000.

   _____

4. Ana ___ her party would be on May 17 2002.

   _____

⭐ Challenge Yourself

What do you think each Challenge Word means? Check the Spelling Dictionary to see if you are right. Then use separate paper to write sentences showing that you understand the meaning of each Challenge Word.

5. I wasn't **jabbing** the window with a stick.

6. Straighten the **crinkled** paper.

7. We **estimated** that we picked up 500 cans.

8. The dog's huge size **stunned** me!

Challenge Words

jabbing
crinkled
estimated
stunned

Unit 4 Review
Lessons 19–23

Use the steps on page 6 to study words that are hard for you.

19

socks
bottle
o'clock
wash

Words with Short o

Write the spelling word that belongs in each group.

1. time, watch, _____

2. jar, can, _____

3. shoes, gloves, _____

4. clean, scrub, _____

20

wrote
hole
know
yellow
goes
November

Words with Long o

Write the spelling word for each clue.

5. This is something you might find in your sock. _____

6. If your shirt is the color of butter, it's this color. _____

7. If you recorded your thoughts on paper, you did this. _____

8. Someone who travels does this. _____

9. If you understand, you do this. _____

10. If it's the eleventh month, it's this month.

_____

21

comb
hello
almost
road
toast

More Words with Long o

Write the spelling word that completes each sentence.

11. Would you like some eggs and _____ for breakfast?

12. The sun was setting, so it was _____ dark outside.

13. I use a _____ and a brush to fix my hair.

14. This _____ goes all the way to Canada.

15. When I see people I know, I say _____ to them.

22

poor
shook
cookies
sure
should

Words with /o͝o/

Write the spelling word that completes each analogy.

16. *Ice cream* is to *freeze* as _____ is to *bake*.

17. *Wake* is to *sleep* as *rich* is to

_____.

18. *Little* is to *small* as _____ is to *must*.

19. *Take* is to *took* as *shake* is to _____.

20. *Thin* is to *skinny* as *certain* is to _____.

23

hoped
shining
stopped
dropped
hopping

More Words with *-ed* or *-ing*

Write the spelling word that is a synonym for each underlined word.

21. The stars were <u>glowing</u> like diamonds.

_____

22. The temperature <u>fell</u> twenty degrees in three hours.

_____

23. Cinderella <u>wished</u> she could go to the ball.

_____

24. Our washing machine <u>quit</u> working yesterday.

_____

25. My little brother was <u>jumping</u> on one foot.

_____

26. /ŏ/ Words

_____

_____

_____

_____

_____

27. /ō/ Words

_____

_____

_____

_____

_____

_____

_____

_____

_____

_____

28. /o͝o/ Words

_____

_____

_____

_____

_____

Review Sort

socks	yellow	should	wrote
know	road	hole	dropped
toast	sure	comb	hello
shook	hopping	stopped	cookies
bottle	goes	poor	hoped
wash	November		

26. Write the **six** short *o* words. Circle the letter that spells /ŏ/ in each word.

27. Write the **eleven** long *o* words. Circle the letter or letters that spell /ō/ in each word.

28. Write the **five** /o͝o/ words. Circle the letter or letters that spell /o͝o/ in each word.

These four words have been sorted into two groups. Explain two ways in which the words in each group are alike.

29. hoped   closed

_____

_____

_____

30. stopped   hopping

_____

_____

_____

Writer's Workshop

A Description

A description tells about a person, a place, or a thing. In description, writers use details that appeal to a reader's senses of sight, hearing, smell, touch, and taste. Here is a part of Ben's description of a baseball game.

The Game

My granddad took me to my first baseball game last summer. It was a perfect day. The sun was bright and yellow. I could smell the green, grassy field. Our seats were right behind home plate. I could hear the thump of the ball in the catcher's mitt. I could see the players' frowns when the umpire called, "You're out!"

Prewriting   To write his description, Ben followed the steps in the writing process. After he decided on a topic, he completed a senses web. On the web, he listed details that appealed to the five senses. The web helped Ben decide which details to include in his description. Part of Ben's senses web is shown here. Study what Ben did.

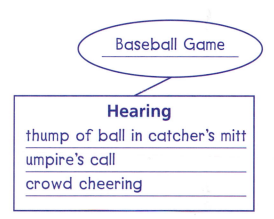

Baseball Game

Hearing

thump of ball in catcher's mitt

umpire's call

crowd cheering

It's Your Turn!

Write your own description. It can be about a place, a person, or anything you can picture clearly in your mind. After you have decided on your topic, make a senses web. Then follow the other steps in the writing process—writing, revising, proofreading, and publishing. Try to use spelling words from this lesson in your description.

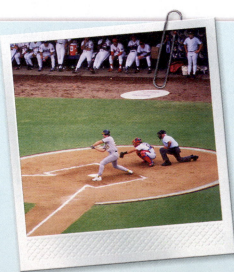

Words with /ōō/ or /yōō/

school

1. oo Words

_____

_____

_____

_____

2. ue, ew Words

_____

_____

_____

_____

_____

_____

3. u-consonant-e Words

_____

_____

_____

4. o, o-consonant-e Words

_____

_____

_____

noon
huge
few
used
tooth
blue
school
Tuesday
who
knew
two
true
too
news
move
June

Say and Listen

Say each spelling word. Listen for the vowel sound you hear in *noon* and *huge*.

Think and Sort

The vowel sound in *noon* and *huge* can be shown as /ōō/. In *huge* and some other /ōō/ words, *y* is pronounced before /ōō/.

Look at the letters in each word. Think about how /ōō/ or /yōō/ is spelled. Spell each word aloud.

1. Write the **four** spelling words with the *oo* pattern.

2. Write the **six** spelling words with the *ue* or *ew* pattern.

3. Write the **three** spelling words with the *u*-consonant-*e* pattern.

4. Write the **three** spelling words with the *o* or *o*-consonant-*e* pattern.

Use the steps on page 6 to study words that are hard for you.

Spelling Patterns

oo	ue	ew
n**oo**n	tr**ue**	n**ew**s

u-consonant-e	o	o-consonant-e
h**u**g**e**	wh**o**	m**o**v**e**

Spelling and Meaning

Classifying   Write the spelling word that belongs in each group.

1. lunch time   twelve o'clock   _____

2. report   information   _____

3. what   where   _____

4. mouth   tongue   _____

5. wiggle   walk   _____

6. post office   library   _____

7. red   green   _____

Clues   Write the spelling word for each clue.

8. one of the summer months   _____

9. not very many   _____

10. the sum of one plus one   _____

11. means the same as *also*   _____

12. gigantic   _____

13. the opposite of *false*   _____

14. not new   _____

15. sounds like *new*   _____

Word Story   The Vikings were people who came to England long ago. One spelling word comes from the word *Tiwesdaeg*. *Tiw* was the name of the Viking war god. *Daeg* meant "day." Write the spelling word that comes from *Tiwesdaeg*.

16. _____

Family Tree: *move*   Think about how the *move* words are alike in spelling and meaning. Then add another *move* word to the tree.

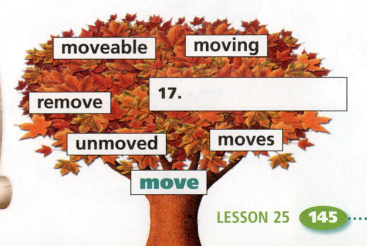

moveable   moving

remove   17.

unmoved   moves

move

Use each spelling word once to complete the story.

The All-School Marathon

_____ was a perfect day for the all-school marathon.
1

The sun was out, but it wasn't _____ hot to run. Jesse
2

_____ he was in good shape. "I should be," he thought.
3

"I've been training all through _____, July, and August."
4

Jesse was new in town. He had moved to Green City late in the

_____ year. He went to his new school for only two
5

weeks. He didn't know anyone. He had met one boy, but it had

been too hard for them to talk. They had met at the dentist's office.

The boy was having a chipped _____ fixed while Jesse
6

was having his teeth cleaned. Jesse had

spent the summer by himself. He had

_____ the summer to get
7

in shape for the race.

It was almost _____
8

when Jesse saw the three-mile marker.

He was among the first ten runners.

He was the only one of them wearing

_____ and white, the
9

colors of his school. "If I win," he

thought, "everybody will know

_____ I am."
10

Jesse pushed on. Only _____ runners were
                                11
in front of him now. He saw the finish line ahead. Then

Jesse made his _____ on the leaders. For a
                        12
_____ yards, they were all neck and neck.
        13

Without warning, Jesse tripped. He fell and scraped his

knee. A _____ crowd gathered around him.
                14
"Did I win or lose?" he asked.

"You finished second," a girl said. "But I've got some

good _____ for you. That's the first time our
            15
school ever came close to winning."

"It's _____," said a boy. "You're the best
            16
runner we've ever had."

Jesse looked up. It was the boy from the dentist's office.
"Remember me?" the boy asked. "My
name is Jack."

Jesse smiled. He had
not won the race, but he
had won a new friend!

noon
huge
few
used
tooth
blue
school
Tuesday
who
knew
two
true
too
news
move
June

Spelling and Writing

noon
huge
few
used
tooth
blue
school
Tuesday
who
knew
two
true
too
news
move
June

Write to the Point

Suppose that you are like Jesse—the new person in school. Help people get to know you. Write a paragraph about yourself. Include details that tell what you like and what you do for fun. Try to use spelling words from this lesson.

Use the strategies on page 7 when you are not sure how to spell a word.

Proofreading

Proofread the journal entry below. Use proofreading marks to correct five spelling mistakes, three capitalization mistakes, and two punctuation mistakes.

Proofreading Marks
◯ spell correctly
≡ capitalize
⊙ add period

June 2

here is the big news for the week. On Toosday I ran in a race at the school track it started at nune and was tue miles long. I wore my green and bloo shirt. Lots of people ran in the race There were adults, children, and grandparents. Uncle Scott came with Mom to see me run. guess whue won. I did!

Dictionary Skills

Pronunciation Most dictionary entries show how a word is said. The way a word is said is called its pronunciation.

Entry Word ⟶ **noon** (nōōn) *noun* Midday; 12 o'clock in the middle of the day: *We'll eat at noon.*

Pronunciation

Letters and symbols are used to write pronunciations. These letters and symbols can be found in the pronunciation key.

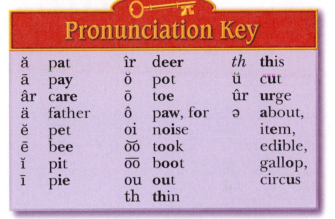

Pronunciation Key

ă	pat	îr	deer	*th*	**this**
ā	pay	ŏ	pot	ŭ	**cut**
âr	**care**	ō	toe	ûr	**urge**
ä	father	ô	paw, for	ə	about,
ĕ	pet	oi	**noise**		item,
ē	bee	ŏŏ	took		edible,
ĭ	pit	ōō	**boot**		gallop,
ī	pie	ou	**out**		circus
		th	**thin**		

Use the pronunciation key to write the word from the boxes that goes with each pronunciation. Check your answers in the Spelling Dictionary.

tooth	move	few	huge

1. /fyōō/ _____

2. /tōōth/ _____

3. /mōōv/ _____

4. /hyōōj/ _____

⭐ Challenge Yourself

Write the Challenge Word for each clue. Check the Spelling Dictionary to see if you are right. Then use separate paper to write sentences showing that you understand the meaning of each Challenge Word.

Challenge Words

pursue	shrewd
casual	dispute

5. T-shirts and jeans are this type of clothing. _____

6. Your teacher can help you with this. _____

7. A clever person is this. _____

8. When you chase someone, you do this to them. _____

Words with /ûr/

bird

List Words

1. **ur Words**

_____

_____

_____

_____

2. **ir Words**

_____

_____

_____

_____

_____

3. **or Words**

_____

_____

_____

_____

4. **ear Words**

_____

_____

5. **ere Word**

_____

curl

world

learn

turn

were

girl

word

bird

work

earth

first

Thursday

dirt

worm

fur

third

Say and Listen

The spelling words for this lesson contain the /ûr/ sounds you hear in *curl*. Say each spelling word. Listen for the /ûr/ sounds.

Think and Sort

Look at the letters in each word. Think about how the /ûr/ sounds are spelled. Spell each word aloud. How many spelling patterns for /ûr/ do you see?

1. Write the **four** spelling words that have the *ur* pattern.

2. Write the **five** spelling words that have the *ir* pattern.

3. Write the **four** spelling words that have the *or* pattern.

4. Write the **two** spelling words that have the *ear* pattern.

5. Write the **one** spelling word that has the *ere* pattern.

Use the steps on page 6 to study words that are hard for you.

Spelling Patterns

ur	ir	or	ear	ere
c**ur**l	f**ir**st	w**or**k	**ear**th	w**ere**

Spelling and Meaning

Definitions   Write the spelling word for each definition. Use the Spelling Dictionary if you need to.

1. a long, thin creature that crawls   _____
2. a young female child   _____
3. the third planet from the sun   _____
4. coming at the beginning   _____
5. next after second   _____
6. to move around   _____
7. the day between Wednesday and Friday   _____
8. a group of letters that has a meaning   _____
9. soil or earth   _____

Synonyms   Write the spelling word that is a synonym for the underlined word in each sentence.

10. Dinosaurs <u>existed</u> on Earth long ago.   _____
11. Next year I hope to <u>study</u> French.   _____
12. We finished our <u>task</u> in the garden.   _____
13. I will <u>loop</u> my hair around my finger.   _____
14. Wouldn't it be fun to go around the <u>earth</u>?   _____
15. Our dog's <u>hair</u> is thick and black.   _____

Word Story   Sometimes the spelling of words changes to make them easier to say or sound nicer. One of the spelling words was once spelled *brid*. Over time, people switched the order of the *r* and *i*. Write the spelling word that shows how *brid* is spelled today.

16. _____

Family Tree: *work*   Think about how the *work* words are alike in spelling and meaning. Then add another *work* word to the tree.

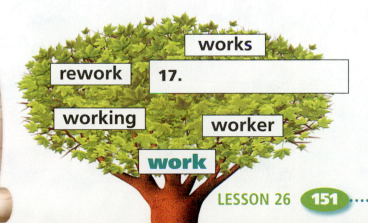

works

rework   17.

working   worker

work

The Bunting

Last _____ my class went to Lone Pine State Park

                    1

for a nature walk. We take these trips to _____ about

                                                        2

nature. Each class trip seems as though it is a holiday.

At the park a _____ named Jane said she would be

                          3

our guide. She told us that keeping the planet healthy is important

_____. We learned lots of interesting facts about the

              4

_____ and sky. Then she told us what plants and

        5

animals to look for. Jane said that we might even see a painted

bunting. A painted bunting is a rare _____ with red,

                                                      6

blue, and green feathers.

We _____ only a little

              7

way down the trail when my friend

Elissa spotted a fawn. It had white

spots on its _____. If only

                          8

I could find something special, too!

I kept my eyes and ears open as I

walked. The path turned once, twice,

and then a _____ time. I happened to look
                      9
down at the _____ beside a tall oak tree.
                     10
At _____ I saw only a wiggly pink
              11
_____. I watched it _____
            12   13
and uncurl. Then I saw one of the most beautiful things

in the _____. I saw a real live painted bunting.
                14
I wanted to yell to the others, but I didn't say a

_____. I didn't want to scare the painted
            15
bunting away.

    I stood as still as a stone and watched the bird hop up to

the tree, then _____ and fly away. In a flash of
                          16
color it was gone. No one else saw the bunting. That was all

right with me. I knew how lucky I had been.

curl
world
learn
turn
were
girl
word
bird
work
earth
first
Thursday
dirt
worm
fur
third

Spelling and Writing

curl
world
learn
turn
were
girl
word
bird
work
earth
first
Thursday
dirt
worm
fur
third

Write to the Point

You don't have to go into the woods to see nature. Look around you. The sky, the trees, and the animals are all part of nature. Write a paragraph telling about one thing you see often in nature. Try to use spelling words from this lesson.

Use the strategies on page 7 when you are not sure how to spell a word.

Proofreading

Proofread this paragraph from a story. Use proofreading marks to correct five spelling mistakes, three capitalization mistakes, and two punctuation mistakes.

Proofreading Marks
◯ spell correctly
≡ capitalize
⊙ add period

Four young robins fluttered to the ground. The first bird ate a werm. the second one ate a bug. The therd bird said bugs made his feathers kurl. he saw a berry in the dert and ate it The fourth bird had work to do. For an hour she dug in the erth. the fifth bird slept late that morning He said it was his day off!

Language Connection

Synonyms and Antonyms   Synonyms are words that have the same meaning. Antonyms are words that have opposite meanings.

> small   little   thick   thin

Write the word from the boxes below that is an antonym of each word.

> dirty   add   huge   young

1. subtract   _____

2. clean   _____

3. tiny   _____

4. old   _____

Each group of four words below has a pair of antonyms and a pair of synonyms. First write the antonyms. Then write the synonyms.

full   turn   empty   spin

5. Antonyms   _____

6. Synonyms   _____

earth   first   world   last

7. Antonyms   _____

8. Synonyms   _____

Challenge Yourself

Use the Spelling Dictionary to answer these questions. Then use separate paper to write sentences showing that you understand the meaning of each Challenge Word.

> **Challenge Words**
> circular   surgeon
> dessert   flourish

9. Is the trunk of a pine tree **circular**?   _____

10. Would you expect to see a **surgeon** in a bird's nest?   _____

11. Would you expect to find grass in a **dessert**?   _____

12. Do some birds **flourish** in wooded areas?   _____

Words with /ä/

barn

Say and Listen

Say each spelling word. Listen for the vowel sound you hear in *dark.*

Think and Sort

Look at the letters in each word. Think about how the vowel sound in *dark* is spelled. Spell each word aloud.

The vowel sound in *dark* can be shown as /ä/. How many spelling patterns for /ä/ do you see?

1. Write the **fifteen** spelling words that have the *a* pattern.

2. Write the **one** spelling word that has the *ea* pattern.

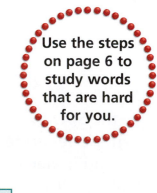

Use the steps on page 6 to study words that are hard for you.

1. *a* Words

_____
_____
_____
_____
_____
_____
_____
_____
_____
_____
_____
_____
_____
_____
_____

2. *ea* Word

_____

dark
yard
art
market
garden
hard
heart
father
March
arm
barn
start
star
card
sharp
bark

Spelling Patterns

a	ea
d**a**rk	h**ea**rt

Spelling and Meaning

Clues Write the spelling word for each clue.

1. where flowers grow _____
2. where to buy fruits and vegetables _____
3. month after February _____
4. what you send on someone's birthday _____
5. where farm animals sleep _____
6. a place to play near a house _____
7. what the inside of a cave is _____
8. what stones are _____
9. another word for *dad* _____
10. the kind of knife you need to cut things _____
11. what the car does when Mom turns the key _____
12. a drawing or painting _____

Multiple Meanings Write the spelling word that has more than one meaning and completes each sentence below.

13. The movie _____ wished upon a shining _____.
14. My _____ pounded as I put all my _____ into the final leg of the race.
15. I heard Scooter _____ at the squirrel gnawing on the tree _____.

Word Story Words that are spelled alike but have different meanings are called **homographs**. One spelling word is a homograph that means "a weapon." The word is also a homograph that names a part of the body. Write the spelling word.

16. _____

Family Tree: *start* Think about how the *start* words are alike in spelling and meaning. Then add another *start* word to the tree.

restart   starts
starter   17.
starting
start

ANNIE OAKLEY

One of the great sharpshooters in Buffalo Bill's Wild West Show was Annie Oakley. Annie was born on a farm in Ohio on August 13, 1860. Annie's mother and _____ had seven children.
1
The family lived in a small log cabin. The forest was their _____. Annie's
2
family shaved the _____ off logs.
3
They used the logs to make furniture.

Annie Oakley

Life on the Oakley farm was _____. The family
4
had to feed all of the animals that lived in the pens and in the
_____. They had to pick the vegetables they grew in
5
their _____. They could not afford to buy many things
6
at a _____. Annie learned to hunt to help feed her
7
family. She became a sharpshooter on the family farm.

Annie put her whole _____ into her work. She
8
often practiced shooting until it was _____. All her
9

hard work helped her become a _____. In 1875
Annie won a shooting contest against champion Frank E.
Butler. Annie and Frank later married.

In _____ of 1884, Annie met Sitting Bull.
Sitting Bull was the chief of the Sioux tribe. Sitting Bull
liked Annie's _____ eyesight and good aim.
He gave her the nickname Little Sure Shot.

Shortly after she got her nickname, Frank and Annie
joined Buffalo Bill's Wild West show. Buffalo Bill used Annie's
sharpshooting act to _____ the show. One
of her most amazing tricks was shooting the thin edge of a
playing _____. She did this while holding a rifle
with only one _____.

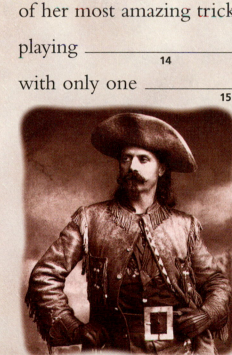

Annie thought sharpshooting
was more than just quick, fancy
shooting. She believed it was an

_____.

Buffalo Bill

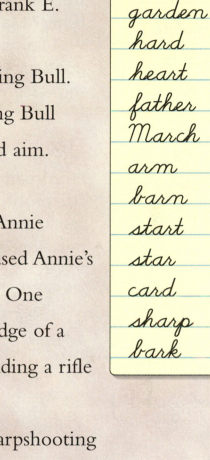

dark
yard
art
market
garden
hard
heart
father
March
arm
barn
start
star
card
sharp
bark

BUFFALO BILL'S WILD WEST SHOW

dark
yard
art
market
garden
hard
heart
father
March
arm
barn
start
star
card
sharp
bark

Write to the Point

Everyone is good at something. Annie Oakley was good at sharpshooting. Are you a good student? A good athlete? A great fisher? Maybe you are a good friend. Write a paragraph telling what you are good at. Try to use spelling words from this lesson in your paragraph.

Use the strategies on page 7 when you are not sure how to spell a word.

Proofreading

Proofread the announcement below. Use proofreading marks to correct five spelling mistakes, three capitalization mistakes, and two punctuation mistakes.

Proofreading Marks
◯ spell correctly
≡ capitalize
? add question mark

Be a Star!

Do you dance or sing Can you do carde tricks? are you good at aret? The Near North neighbors are having a talent show. We will steart practicing next week. we also need someone to paint signs. The show will end with a parade around the Near North Park flower gardin. Would you like to join us Come to mary Wu's yarde on Friday after school!

Dictionary Skills

Multiple Meanings   Some words have more than one meaning. Look at the entry for *heart* from the Spelling Dictionary. The word *heart* has two meanings. Each is numbered. Read the sample sentence for each meaning of *heart*. The words around the word *heart* give a clue to its meaning.

> **heart** (härt) *noun, plural* **hearts**
> **1.** The organ in the chest that pumps blood through the body: *The doctor listened to my heart.* **2.** Courage and enthusiasm: *He put his heart into winning the game.*

Write **Meaning 1** or **Meaning 2** to indicate which definition of *heart* is used in each sentence. Then write your own sentences showing you understand each meaning of *heart*.

1. Our class lost **heart** when we lost the game.   _____

2. My **heart** beats fast after a race.   _____

_____

_____

Challenge Yourself

What do you think each Challenge Word means? Check the Spelling Dictionary to see if you are right. Then use separate paper to write sentences showing that you understand the meaning of each Challenge Word.

Challenge Words	
carton	starch
artistic	barbecue

3. You can buy milk in a **carton** or a jug.

4. A lot of **starch** on your shirt will make it stiff.

5. Annie Oakley thought that sharpshooting was **artistic**.

6. My sister served **barbecue** at her wedding.

Words with /oi/

boil

1. *oi* Words

_____
_____
_____
_____
_____
_____
_____
_____
_____
_____
_____

2. *oy* Words

_____
_____
_____
_____
_____

coin
boy
choice
spoil
royal
boil
voice
toy
soil
joy
noise
point
broil
enjoy
join
oil

Say and Listen

Say each spelling word. Listen for the vowel sound you hear in *coin*.

Think and Sort

Look at the letters in each word. Think about how the vowel sound in *coin* is spelled. Spell each word aloud.

The vowel sound in *coin* can be shown as /oi/. How many spelling patterns for /oi/ do you see?

1. Write the **eleven** spelling words that have the *oi* pattern.

2. Write the **five** spelling words that have the *oy* pattern.

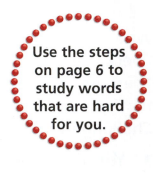

Use the steps on page 6 to study words that are hard for you.

Spelling Patterns

oi	oy
c**oi**n	t**oy**

Spelling and Meaning

Classifying   Write the spelling word that belongs in each group of words.

1. noble   kingly   _____
2. gas   coal   _____
3. doll   yo-yo   _____
4. happiness   pleasure   _____
5. sound   speech   _____
6. rot   decay   _____
7. tie   connect   _____
8. money   dollar bill   _____

Analogies   Write the spelling word that completes each analogy.

9. *Man* is to *woman* as _____ is to *girl*.

10. *Laugh* is to _____ as *cry* is to *fear*.

11. *Lose* is to *loss* as *choose* is to _____.

12. *Soft* is to *whisper* as *loud* is to _____.

13. *Ocean* is to *sea* as _____ is to *dirt*.

14. *Cake* is to *bake* as *steak* is to _____.

15. *Finger* is to _____ as *hand* is to *wave*.

Word Story   This spelling word tells what happens when a liquid gets very hot. It comes from the Latin word *bulla*. *Bulla* meant "bubble." When a liquid gets very hot, we can see large bubbles in it. The bubbles move around very quickly. Write the word.

16. _____

Family Tree: *joy*   Think about how the *joy* words are alike in spelling and meaning. Then add another *joy* word to the tree.

enjoyment

enjoy

17.

joyful

joys

joy

Use each spelling word once to complete the story.

A Camping Tale

Liza was full of _____ when she caught the fish. But
1

soon after that, she realized that she was alone. She yelled until she almost

lost her _____. But no one answered. She was lost. There
2

was no one to _____ the way back to camp. Her camping
3

trip had become a nightmare.

"I might not _____ it," she thought, "but I guess I'll have
4

to make it alone. I don't have any other _____!"
5

At first Liza jumped at every _____ in the woods. But
6

soon she got used to the noises. She was very hungry. At least she had a

few supplies in her backpack. She would be all right.

"The first thing I'll do," she thought, "is build a fire. It will keep me nice

and warm. Then I'll _____ some water for cocoa. I don't have
7

any _____ to fry the fish, but that's all right.
8

I think I can _____ it over the fire. I'll cook a
                        9
_____ feast!"
        10

Liza gathered some wood and put it in a little pile. Then she realized that she needed matches. She put her hand in her right jeans pocket but found only an old _____. Then she
                                                          11
tried the other pocket. She found her yo-yo. "I don't think a

_____ will help me start a fire," she said aloud.
        12
Then she looked through her backpack. She found the matches at the bottom of it and lit the wood. Soon she had a little fire going.

Liza had just finished broiling the fish when it began to rain. She didn't want the rain to _____ her dinner. She
                                          13
pushed a branch into the soft _____. Then she put
                                        14
her jacket over it to make a kind of tent. She ate her fish and listened to the rain. She began to yawn. Soon she was fast asleep.

When she woke up, a _____ was looking into
                              15
the tent. It was her brother. "Breakfast is

ready," he said. "Aren't you going

to _____ us?"
        16

Liza was in her family's

tent. It was a bright morning.

The birds were singing. She

laughed. Her nightmare

camping trip was only a dream.

coin
boy
choice
spoil
royal
boil
voice
toy
soil
joy
noise
point
broil
enjoy
join
oil

Spelling and Writing

coin
boy
choice
spoil
royal
boil
voice
toy
soil
joy
noise
point
broil
enjoy
join
oil

Write to the Point

Think about the things people do on camping trips. Then continue a "A Camping Tale" by writing a paragraph telling what Liza did after breakfast. Try to use spelling words from this lesson in your paragraph.

Use the strategies on page 7 when you are not sure how to spell a word.

Proofreading

Proofread the e-mail below. Use proofreading marks to correct five spelling mistakes, three capitalization mistakes, and two punctuation mistakes.

Proofreading Marks
- ◯ spell correctly
- ≡ capitalize
- ⊙ add period

| **e-mail** |
| Address Book | Attachment | Check Spelling | Send | Save Draft | Cancel |

Diego,

Last night I dreamed I lived in a royle castle. I had every toy a boy could want What I had for breakfast, lunch, and dinner was my choic. nothing could spoyal my joi Then I heard a noise. It was the voyce of my brother, james. It was so loud that it woke me up.

Have you ever had a dream like this? I would enjoy reading about it. send me an e-mail.

Tomas

Language Connection

Capital Letters   The following kinds of words begin with a capital letter:

> • the first word of a sentence   • the names of streets
>
> • the names of people and pets   • the names of cities and states

Write each sentence below, using capital letters correctly. Circle the spelling word in the sentence.

1. we will enjoy visiting minneapolis.

_____

2. my dog max makes a lot of noise!

_____

3. can you point out mallory street?

_____

4. this coin was made in colorado.

_____

5. mrs. hays bought a toy for her baby.

_____

6. kevin and I want to join the baseball team.

_____

Challenge Yourself

Use the Spelling Dictionary to answer these questions. Then use separate paper to write sentences showing that you understand the meaning of each Challenge Word.

Challenge Words

moisten

poisonous

rejoice

enjoyment

7. Do people ever **moisten** stamps?

_____

8. Are **poisonous** snakes dangerous?   _____

9. Does Liza **rejoice** when she realizes she is lost?   _____

10. Does a nightmare usually bring **enjoyment**?   _____

More Contractions

Please don't feed the birds

don't

1. Two Words

_____
_____
_____
_____
_____
_____
_____
_____
_____
_____
_____
_____
_____
_____
_____

2. One Word

_____

isn't
weren't
can't
doesn't
hadn't
mustn't
wouldn't
won't
shouldn't
aren't
wasn't
don't
couldn't
didn't
hasn't
haven't

Say and Listen

Say the spelling words. Listen for the sounds at the end of each word.

Think and Sort

All of the spelling words in this lesson are contractions. Each contraction is formed from the word *not* joined with another word. When the two words are joined, one or more letters are left out. An apostrophe (') is used to show the missing letters.

In the contraction *won't,* the spelling of *will* changes to *wo.* One contraction, *can't,* is formed from one word, not two separate words.

1. Write the **fifteen** spelling words that are formed from *not* joined with a separate word.

2. Write the **one** spelling word that is formed from one word.

Use the steps on page 6 to study words that are hard for you.

Spelling Patterns

is + not	will + not	cannot
isn't	won't	can't

Spelling and Meaning

Either . . . or   Write the spelling word that completes each sentence.

1. Either Wags will or he _____.
2. Either you do or you _____.
3. Either James could or he _____.
4. Either Julie would or she _____.
5. Either Sara does or she _____.
6. Either Ricky was or he _____.

Trading Places   Write the contraction that can be used instead of the underlined word or words in each sentence.

7. Marta <u>had not</u> seen the new puppy.   _____

8. You <u>must not</u> touch the wet paint.   _____

9. Lan <u>did not</u> bring his lunch.   _____

10. I <u>cannot</u> believe you ran five miles!   _____

11. The mail <u>has not</u> come yet.   _____

12. I <u>have not</u> finished my homework.   _____

13. Did you know that whales <u>are not</u> fish?   _____

14. We <u>were not</u> home on Saturday.   _____

15. "That <u>is not</u> my car," Ms. Ford said.   _____

Word Story   One of the spelling words is a form of the word *shall*. First it was spelled *sceolde*. Then the spelling changed to *shollde*. Now it is spelled another way. Write the spelling word that is a form of this word plus *not*.

16. _____

Family Tree: *haven't*   *Haven't* is a contraction of *have* and *not*. Think about how the *have* words are alike in spelling and meaning. Then add another *have* word to the tree.

having

had

17.

has

haven't

have

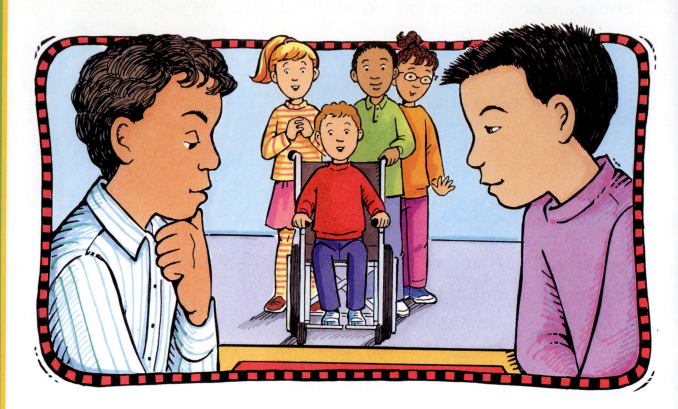

The Challenge

Max watched Hector nervously, waiting to see what Hector would do next. This was the first time he had faced Hector. Max _____ happy about it. "If only I _____
1   2
said yes to his challenge," he thought. "Then I _____
3
be in this mess."

"You _____ going to back down?" Hector asked.
4
Max knew in his heart that he could not back down now. He just _____. A lot of his friends were watching him. They
5
_____ going to leave until it was all over. They had
6
tried to tell him about Hector. "You _____ heard?"
7
they had asked. "He's tough. He _____ ever lose."
8

Max _____ like to lose. His hands were
9
sweaty. His knees were shaking. "I _____ help
10
it," he thought. "I want to beat this guy."

Max rubbed his hands on his jeans. "Calm down," he
told himself. "Whatever happens, I _____ look
11
scared. I _____ want to make it easy for Hector
12
to win. Besides, it really _____ be the end of
13
the world if I lose."

Then Hector made his move. Max knew that it was the
wrong one. "He _____ got a chance now!" he
14
thought. Max grinned. "You _____ have done
15
that, Hector," he said. "I'm going to beat you. But don't
worry. It _____ going to hurt for long."
16
In one move Max cleared the checkerboard of Hector's
pieces. The game was over.

Hector shook Max's
hand and smiled. "You play
a good game of checkers," he
said. "I think I like playing
with you."

Max smiled back. He had
met the challenge.

isn't
weren't
can't
doesn't
hadn't
mustn't
wouldn't
won't
shouldn't
aren't
wasn't
don't
couldn't
didn't
hasn't
haven't

Spelling and Writing

isn't
weren't
can't
doesn't
hadn't
mustn't
wouldn't
won't
shouldn't
aren't
wasn't
don't
couldn't
didn't
hasn't
haven't

Write to the Point

Rules tell how to play a game and what players can and cannot do. For example, one soccer rule is "Don't touch the ball with your hands." Write three rules for a game you know. Try to use spelling words from this lesson in your rules.

> Use the strategies on page 7 when you are not sure how to spell a word.

Proofreading

Proofread the note below. Use proofreading marks to correct five spelling mistakes, three capitalization mistakes, and two unnecessary words.

Proofreading Marks
- ◯ spell correctly
- ≡ capitalize
- ℓ take out

Chad,

I couldnt' wait for you to see this game.

Open the box and look at the checkerboard. it

has'nt been used in in ten years. It's still in great

shape! Wouldent you like to play? Well, Aunt rose

won'nt let anyone use it except me and one other

person. you are that person. I'll come to your

house tonight for a game. Doesnt' that sound like

like a great plan?

Ling

Language Connection

Be Verbs There are many different forms of the verb *be*. Some tell what is happening now. Others tell what happened in the past. These forms of *be* are used in *not* contractions.

Present Tense		Contraction
is	The bus **is** late.	**isn't**
are	They **are** in a hurry.	**aren't**

Past Tense		Contraction
was	Bart **was** still here.	**wasn't**
were	Jill and Will **were** on the way.	**weren't**

Use the correct contraction above to complete each sentence.

1. Toni _____ here every day.

2. Today the trains _____ on time.

3. Paige and LaWanda _____ here last Thursday.

4. Last month _____ the best month for planting a garden.

⭐ Challenge Yourself

Use the Spelling Dictionary to answer these questions. Then use separate paper to write sentences showing that you understand the meaning of each Challenge Word.

Challenge Words

there'll	how'd
we'd	there'd

5. Is **there'll** a contraction for the words *there will*?

_____

6. Is **how'd** a contraction for the words *how did*? _____

7. Is **we'd** a contraction for *we did*? _____

8. Is **there'd** a contraction for the words *there did*? _____

Unit 5 Review
Lessons 25–29

Use the steps on page 6 to study words that are hard for you.

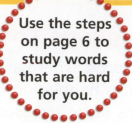

25

too
true
knew
few
huge
used
two

Words with /ōō/ or /yōō/

Write the spelling word that can be used instead of the word or words in dark type in each sentence.

1. The story that we read was **real**. _____

2. My father's car is **not new**. _____

3. The sun is **very** hot in the summer. _____

4. **One plus one** is less than three. _____

5. Malika **was certain** that she would win. _____

6. **Not very many** people stood in line. _____

7. Elephants and whales are **big**. _____

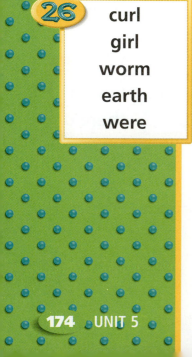

26

curl
girl
worm
earth
were

Words with /ûr/

Write the spelling word that belongs in each group.

8. lady   woman   _____

9. are   was   _____

10. curve   coil   _____

11. soil   ground   _____

12. snake   eel   _____

27

garden
father
sharp
heart

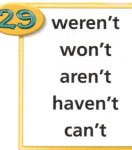

Words with /ä/

Write the spelling word that completes each analogy.

13. *Scissors* is to _____ as *feather* is to *soft*.

14. *Son* is to _____ as *daughter* is to *mother*.

15. *Apple* is to *orchard* as *carrot* is to _____.

16. *Brain* is to *head* as _____ is to *chest*.

28

voice
soil
enjoy
royal

Words with /oi/

Write the spelling word for each clue.

17. People sing with this. _____

18. This is a synonym for *like*.

_____

19. Kings and queens are this.

_____

20. People plant seeds in this.

_____

29

weren't
won't
aren't
haven't
can't

More Contractions

Write the contractions for the words.

21. cannot _____

22. are + not _____

23. have + not _____

24. will + not _____

25. were + not _____

26. /o͞o/ or /yo͞o/ Words

_____

_____

_____

_____

_____

27. /ûr/ Words

_____

_____

_____

_____

_____

28. /ä/ Words

_____

_____

_____

_____

29. /oi/ Words

_____

_____

_____

Review Sort

worm	girl	royal	knew
true	heart	huge	curl
sharp	enjoy	garden	were
soil	earth	father	few
too	used	voice	

26. Write the **six** /o͞o/ or /yo͞o/ words. Circle the letters that spell /o͞o/ or /yo͞o/ in each word.

27. Write the **five** /ûr/ words. Circle the letters that spell /ûr/ in each word.

28. Write the **four** /ä/ words. Circle the letter or letters that spell /ä/ in each word.

29. Write the **four** /oi/ words. Circle the letters that spell /oi/ in each word.

These six words have been sorted into two groups. Explain how the words in each group are alike.

30. hasn't   haven't   hadn't

_____

_____

31. doesn't   don't   didn't

_____

_____

Writer's Workshop

A How-To Paragraph

A how-to paragraph tells how to do something. In a how-to paragraph, writers give step-by-step directions, using order words such as *first, second, next, then,* and *finally.* Here is part of Alicia's how-to paragraph. In it she tells how to make a kind of sandwich.

How to Make a Super Sandwich

A Super Sandwich is a tasty treat. Here's how to make it. First, get some bread, peanut butter, honey, and bananas. Second, cut the bananas into very thin slices. Next, spread the peanut butter on two slices of bread. Then, pour a little honey on the peanut butter.

Prewriting   To write her how-to paragraph, Alicia followed the steps in the writing process. She began with a Prewriting activity. She used a how-to chart to list the steps for making her favorite snack. This helped her know the order in which to write the steps. Part of Alicia's how-to chart is shown here. Study what Alicia did.

1. Get two slices of bread, peanut butter, honey, bananas.

2. Cut the bananas.

3. Spread the peanut butter on the bread.

It's Your Turn!

Get ready to write your own how-to paragraph. Think of something you know how to do. After you have decided what to write about, make a how-to chart. Then follow the other steps in the writing process—writing, revising, proofreading, and publishing. Try to use spelling words from this lesson in your how-to paragraph.

Words with /ô/

frog

1. o Words

_____
_____
_____
_____
_____
_____

2. a Words

_____
_____
_____
_____
_____
_____

3. ough Words

_____
_____

4. au Word

_____

5. aw Word

_____

draw
walk
bought
because
frog
along
long
water
always
brought
off
belong
mall
strong
tall
talk

Say and Listen

Say each spelling word. Listen for the vowel sound you hear in *draw*.

Think and Sort

Look at the letters in each word. Think about how the vowel sound in *draw* is spelled. Spell each word aloud.

The vowel sound in *draw* can be shown as /ô/. How many spelling patterns for /ô/ do you see?

1. Write the **six** spelling words that have the *o* pattern.

2. Write the **six** spelling words that have the *a* pattern.

3. Write the **two** spelling words that have the *ough* pattern.

4. Write the **one** spelling word that has the *au* pattern.

5. Write the **one** spelling word that has the *aw* pattern.

Use the steps on page 6 to study words that are hard for you.

Spelling Patterns

o	a	ough	au	aw
l**o**ng	t**a**lk	b**ough**t	bec**au**se	dr**aw**

Spelling and Meaning

Antonyms Write the spelling word that is an antonym of each underlined word.

1. That basketball player is very <u>short</u>. _____

2. Please turn <u>on</u> the light. _____

3. Tina <u>never</u> eats breakfast. _____

4. Elephants are very large and <u>weak</u>. _____

5. Mr. Good gave a <u>brief</u> speech. _____

Clues Write the spelling word for each clue.

6. what you do on the phone _____

7. what people and animals drink _____

8. place to shop _____

9. past tense of *bring* _____

10. what artists do _____

11. green thing that sits on a lily pad _____

12. means "to be owned by" _____

13. means almost the same as *beside* _____

14. rhymes with *talk* _____

15. past tense of *buy* _____

Word Story People used to say that a dish broke "by cause" it fell. Later, they made one word of *by* and *cause*. Write the word as it is spelled today.

16. _____

Family Tree: *talk* Think about how the *talk* words are alike in spelling and meaning. Then add another *talk* word to the tree.

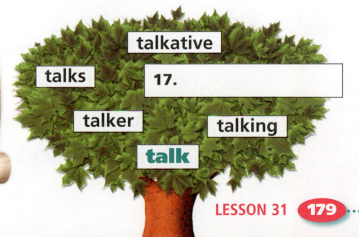

talkative

talks

17.

talker

talking

talk

The Frog Prince

Libby's older sister, Rachel, liked to

_____ pictures. One day she
         1

drew a picture of a green _____.
                                      2

It had a little gold crown on its head. Rachel

_____ the picture to Libby.
        3

Rachel could not hear, so the two girls used their hands to talk to

each other. "If you find a frog, it might turn into a prince," Rachel

signed to Libby with her hands. Libby had a _____
                                                         4

feeling that Rachel was teasing her.

"That's just silly _____," Libby signed back. But not
                              5

_____ after, she wondered what would happen if a frog
        6

could turn into a prince. Would he be short or _____?
                                                             7

Would he be kind and fun? Libby thought about what she would say

to a frog prince.

"Aren't you ready yet?" Mom called. Libby's daydream ended.

Sometimes Libby's mom spent Saturday afternoon shopping at the

_____. Libby _____ went. Rachel usually
        8   9

came _____, too. Today at the mall, Mom and Rachel
          10

just _____ a snack. Libby wanted to be by herself. She
        11

decided to _____ around the mall.
                  12

It was warm, so Libby took _____ her jacket. But
                                         13

she was still hot. "Maybe it's cooler by the _____," she
                                                          14

thought. Libby walked to the pond in the center of the mall. She sat down on the low wall around the pond. Suddenly a frog jumped to the wall and sat beside her.

"Could it be a prince?" Libby wondered. As she reached for the frog, a voice yelled, "Leave that frog alone! It doesn't _____ to you!"

₁₅

Mr. Muller, the pet store owner, rushed over. "What are you doing to my frog?" he asked. "I've been searching for him everywhere."

"Nothing at all," Libby replied. "I just wanted to help him _____ he might be . . ." She stopped. It

₁₆

sounded so silly. She got up and quickly walked away.

"Now I'll never be sure," Libby thought as she went to look for her mom and Rachel.

draw
walk
bought
because
frog
along
long
water
always
brought
off
belong
mall
strong
tall
talk

Spelling and Writing

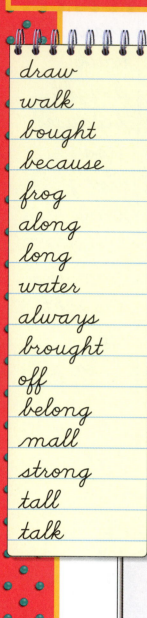

draw
walk
bought
because
frog
along
long
water
always
brought
off
belong
mall
strong
tall
talk

Write to the Point

Do you think a prince would have appeared if Libby had kissed the frog? Write a new ending for the story. Start your paragraph with "Libby reached for the frog, and _____." Try to use spelling words from this lesson in your ending.

Use the strategies on page 7 when you are not sure how to spell a word.

Proofreading

Proofread the e-mail below. Use proofreading marks to correct five spelling mistakes, four capitalization mistakes, and two unnecessary words.

Proofreading Marks
◯ spell correctly
≡ capitalize
✓ take out

---

e-mail

| Address Book | Attachment | Check Spelling | Send | Save Draft | Cancel |

Dear Aunt jane,

   Mom and i miss you. We allways go to the park.

We tawk as we walk down the path by the watter.

it's nice becuz we're together. We wish you you

could come aloong with us. we want to have a

picnic by the duck pond. I need you to help me me

catch a frog, too. Will you come to visit us soon?

Libby

Language Connection

Subject and Predicate The subject of a sentence tells who or what is doing the action or being talked about. The predicate of a sentence tells what the subject does or did.

Subject	Predicate
Sally	danced.
The cat	had jumped off the chair.

Unscramble the spelling words as you write the sentences below. Then circle the subjects and underline the predicates.

1. My sister hid behind a latl tree.

_____

2. Ling tughob a baseball.

_____

3. Mrs. Martinez took a nogl vacation.

_____

4. I will wrad a picture of you.

_____

5. The old clock fell fof the shelf.

_____

Challenge Yourself

Use the Spelling Dictionary to answer these questions. Then use separate paper to write sentences showing that you understand the meaning of each Challenge Word.

Challenge Words

sausage	broth
dawdle	install

6. Should you comb your hair with a **sausage**? _____

7. Could you find **broth** in vegetable soup? _____

8. If you were in a hurry, would you **dawdle**? _____

9. Should you **install** a stove before you turn it on? _____

More Words with /ô/

storm

Spelling List

1. au Words

_____

_____

2. o Words

_____

_____

_____

_____

_____

_____

_____

_____

_____

3. oo, ou Words

_____

_____

_____

_____

4. a Word

_____

August

morning

four

quart

pour

popcorn

before

autumn

corner

storm

door

floor

north

born

fork

sport

Say and Listen

Say each spelling word. Listen for the first vowel sound you hear in *August* and *morning*.

Think and Sort

Look at the letters in each word. Think about how the first vowel sound in *August* and *morning* is spelled. Spell each word aloud.

The first vowel sound in *August* and *morning* can be shown as /ô/. How many spelling patterns for /ô/ do you see?

1. Write the **two** spelling words that have the *au* pattern.

2. Write the **nine** spelling words that have the *o* pattern.

3. Write the **four** spelling words that have the *oo* or *ou* pattern.

4. Write the **one** spelling word that has the *a* pattern.

Use the steps on page 6 to study words that are hard for you.

Spelling Patterns

au	o	oo	ou	a
A**u**gust	m**o**rning	d**oo**r	f**ou**r	qu**a**rt

Spelling and Meaning

Clues Write the spelling word for each clue.

1. snack to eat at the movies _____
2. spoon, knife, _____ _____
3. rain or snow and lots of wind _____
4. where the walls in a room meet _____
5. how to get milk into a glass _____

Analogies Write the spelling word that completes each analogy.

6. *East* is to *west* as _____ is to *south*.
7. *Summer* is to *winter* as *spring* is to _____.
8. *Evening* is to *dinner* as _____ is to *breakfast*.
9. *Cool* is to *warm* as *after* is to _____.
10. *Foot* is to *yard* as _____ is to *gallon*.
11. *Above* is to *below* as *ceiling* is to _____.
12. *Lid* is to *jar* as _____ is to *house*.
13. *One* is to *two* as *three* is to _____.
14. *Color* is to *blue* as _____ is to *hockey*.
15. *Bird* is to *hatch* as *child* is to _____.

Word Story Caesar Augustus was one of the greatest Roman emperors. *Augustus* meant "very great man." Caesar Augustus had the Romans name a month after him. This month still has his name. Write the spelling word that names this month.

16. _____

Family Tree: *north* Think about how the *north* words are alike in spelling and meaning. Then add another *north* word to the tree.

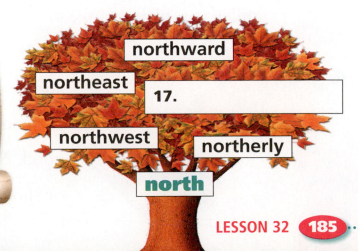

northward

northeast

17.

northwest

northerly

north

Use each spelling word once to complete the selection.

Happy Hiking

Hiking is a great _____ for families to enjoy together. Here are some easy tips to make hiking safe and fun for everyone.

Find and wear good hiking boots. Remember that your legs and feet will be doing a lot of work. Break in brand new boots _____ going hiking. Wear them around on your living room _____ first so that your feet won't hurt on the trail later.

Before you go out your front _____ and head for the trail, make sure you and your family members pack plenty of supplies. You should also carry water. Each person will need one _____ of water for each _____ or five miles you plan to hike.

Pack lots of healthful snacks as well. Fruit and granola bars make good snacks. Freshly popped and unsalted _____ is also good. You won't need a _____ or spoon to eat it, either.

You and your family should also protect yourselves from the sun. Wear a hat with a wide brim. Remember to put on lots of sunblock. You can get a sunburn on cool days in the spring or in the _____ as well as on hot

9

summer days in _____. You should also take a

10

raincoat in case rain starts to _____. Remember

11

that a _____ can blow in at any time.

12

Learn how to use a compass. A compass needle always points to the _____. Keep in mind, too, that

13

in the _____ the sun is always in the east. If you

14

remember these two things, you will not get lost.

Be kind to any animals you see. Never back a wild animal into a _____. Make noises to let animals know

15

where you are. It is especially important to avoid disturbing baby animals that have just been _____. Angry

16

animal parents can be dangerous!

Finally, stay with your family. Never go off by yourself. Stay together and help one another. Remembering these tips can help make your family hiking trip the best ever!

August
morning
four
quart
pour
popcorn
before
autumn
corner
storm
door
floor
north
born
fork
sport

Spelling and Writing

August
morning
four
quart
pour
popcorn
before
autumn
corner
storm
door
floor
north
born
fork
sport

Write to the Point

Write a paragraph that tells younger children things that will help them prepare for a hiking or other outdoor trip. Tell what to bring and how to be safe. Try to use spelling words from this lesson.

Use the strategies on page 7 when you are not sure how to spell a word.

Proofreading

Proofread the paragraph below. Use proofreading marks to correct five spelling mistakes, three capitalization mistakes, and two punctuation mistakes.

Proofreading Marks

◯ spell correctly
≡ capitalize
⊙ add period

Hiking is a great spoort. It can be a lot of fun. here are some things to remember when you go Make sure you are wearing good shoes. Befour you go, put water and snacks in a backpack Trail mix and popcawrn are good snacks. also, bring rain gear in case there is a stourm. It's a good idea to start early in the morening, when you have lots of energy. As you hike along, remember to stop and rest. you will have more fun if you don't get too tired.

Dictionary Skills

Alphabetical Order Many words begin with the same letter or the same two letters. To put these words in alphabetical order, use the third letter of each word. Look at the two words below.

train	trim

Both words start with the letters *tr.* To put them in alphabetical order, look at the third letter. The third letter in *train* is *a.* The third letter in *trim* is *i.* In the alphabet, *a* comes before *i,* so *train* comes before *trim.*

In each list below, the words begin with the same two letters. Look at the third letter of each word. Then write the words in alphabetical order.

1. autumn   aunt   August

_____

_____

_____

2. porch   point   pour

_____

_____

_____

3. fond   four   foggy

_____

_____

_____

4. money   morning   moon

_____

_____

_____

Challenge Yourself

Write the Challenge Word for each clue. Check the Spelling Dictionary to see if you are right. Then use separate paper to write sentences showing that you understand the meaning of each Challenge Word.

Challenge Words	
ornament	wharf
coarse	corridor

5. You can expect to see water and boats at this. _____

6. You walk through this to get to another part of a building.

_____

7. This is a kind of decoration. _____

8. This word describes things that are not smooth. _____

Words with /ou/

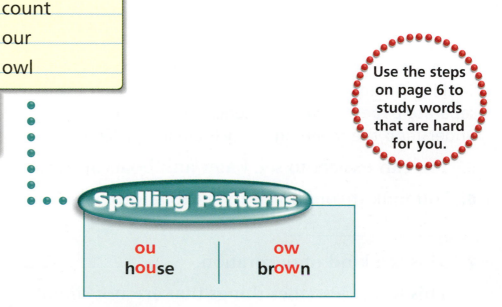

tower

1. *ou* Words

_____
_____
_____
_____
_____
_____
_____
_____
_____

2. *ow* Words

_____
_____
_____
_____
_____
_____
_____

house
flower
town
sound
ground
tower
found
brown
about
hour
power
down
around
count
our
owl

Say and Listen

Say each spelling word. Listen for the vowel sound you hear in *house.*

Think and Sort

Look at the letters in each word. Think about how the vowel sound in *house* is spelled. Spell each word aloud.

The vowel sound in *house* can be shown as /ou/. How many spelling patterns for /ou/ do you see?

1. Write the **nine** spelling words that have the *ou* pattern.

2. Write the **seven** spelling words that have the *ow* pattern.

Use the steps on page 6 to study words that are hard for you.

Spelling Patterns

ou	ow
h**ou**se	br**ow**n

Spelling and Meaning

Hink Pinks   Hink pinks are pairs of rhyming words that have funny meanings. Read each clue. Write the spelling word that completes each hink pink.

1. a place for mice to live   mouse _____
2. a beagle's bark   hound _____
3. the time to bake   flour _____
4. rain falling on a tall building   _____ shower
5. a night bird's loud sound   _____ howl

Letter Scramble   Unscramble the letters in parentheses. Then write the spelling word to complete the phrase.

6. (wodn)   run _____ the hill
7. (repow)   _____ from electricity
8. (boaut)   books for and _____ children
9. (wolfer)   a _____ in a vase
10. (ungord)   on the _____ or in the air
11. (dnofu)   lost and _____
12. (nuoct)   _____ to ten
13. (wonrb)   _____ hair and eyes
14. (ruodna)   in, _____, and through
15. (rou)   her, their, and _____

Word Story   In Old English a fence or a wall was called a *toun*. A fence or wall became a sign that people lived nearby. The place where people lived became known as a *toun*. Write the spelling word that comes from *toun*.

16. _____

Family Tree: *power*   Think about how the *power* words are alike in spelling and meaning. Then add another *power* word to the tree.

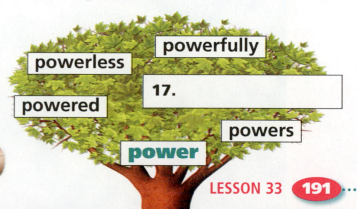

powerfully

powerless

17.

powered

powers

power

Use each spelling word once to complete the selection.

Owls

Of all the birds, the _____ is one of the easiest to
1
recognize. An owl has a large, round head. It has big eyes that
look straight ahead.

Owls come in several colors. Snowy owls are white. Owls of
the deep rain forest are often dark _____ in color. At
2
last _____, there were _____ 130 different
3   4
kinds of owls. Scientists think that some owls are in danger of
becoming extinct. They feel it is _____ duty to
5
protect the owl. Owls are not only beautiful. They are also useful
to people. Owls help farmers. They eat rodents that hurt crops.

Owls can be _____ almost everywhere in the
6
world. Some owls make their home in a tree or in a barn. Some

▲ long-eared owl

◀ crested owl

owls have even nested on top of a water _____ 7 near a busy _____ 8 .

Most owls hunt for food at night. Their eyes are large, so they see well in the dark. Owls also have very good hearing. Using their sharp hearing and keen sight, they fly above the _____ 9 , looking for small animals such as mice and rats. Owls are meat eaters. They never nibble on leaves or the petals of a _____ 10 .

An owl can swoop _____ 11 without making a _____ 12 . Once caught, an animal has little chance of getting away from the _____ 13 of the owl's grip. In one _____ 14 an owl can catch two or three mice.

Owls are as good at catching mice as cats are. But owls do not make good _____ 15 pets. Owls need room to fly _____ 16 . The best way to enjoy owls is to watch them in the wild.

house
flower
town
sound
ground
tower
found
brown
about
hour
power
down
around
count
our
owl

snowy owl ▶

▲ great grey owl

Spelling and Writing

house
flower
town
sound
ground
tower
found
brown
about
hour
power
down
around
count
our
owl

Write to the Point

An owl does not make a very good pet. Owls need space to fly and look for food. However, many other animals do make good pets. Write a paragraph telling which animal you think makes the best pet and why. Try to use spelling words from this lesson.

Use the strategies on page 7 when you are not sure how to spell a word.

Proofreading

Proofread the journal entry below. Use proofreading marks to correct five spelling mistakes, three capitalization mistakes, and two unnecessary words.

Proofreading Marks
◯ spell correctly
≡ capitalize
ℓ take out

May 14

Today was a wild day! Dad and I heard a strange sownd. we looked around the inside of the howse. Then we looked outside. Finally we climbed up on the roof. We found an owel stuck in our our chimney. Dad got his gloves and a fishing net. it took us an hour to free the big broun bird, but it seemed all right as it flew away. I can't wait to to tell chris abuot it.

Using the Spelling Table

A spelling table can help you find the spelling of a word in a dictionary. Suppose you are not sure how the vowel sound in *should* is spelled. You can use a spelling table to find the different spellings for the sound. First, find the pronunciation symbol for the sound. Then read the first spelling listed for /ŏŏ/ and look up *shoold* in the dictionary. Look for each spelling in the dictionary until you find the correct one.

Sound	Spellings	Examples
/ŏŏ/	oo ou u u_e	book, could, pull, sure

Write the correct spelling for each word. Use the Spelling Table on page 213 and the Spelling Dictionary. One word has two correct spellings.

1. /brôth/ _____

2. /mān tān′/ _____

3. /ăd mīr′/ _____

4. /dōm/ _____

5. /fīr/ _____

6. /wīr/ _____

7. /stärch/ _____

8. /dîr/ _____ _____

Challenge Yourself

What do you think each Challenge Word means? Check the Spelling Dictionary to see if you are right. Then use separate paper to write sentences showing that you understand the meaning of each Challenge Word.

Challenge Words

doubtful
devour
bough
wildflower

9. It is **doubtful** that an owl would be a good house pet.

10. A hungry owl will **devour** a big meal.

11. A little owl sat on the **bough** of a tree.

12. An owl would rather eat a mouse than a **wildflower**.

Words with /îr/, /âr/, or /īr/

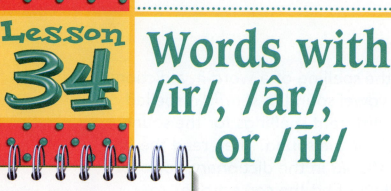

deer

1. /îr/ Words

_____
_____
_____
_____
_____
_____

2. /âr/ Words

_____
_____
_____
_____
_____
_____

3. /īr/ Words

_____
_____
_____

near
care
fire
where
hear
wire
stairs
deer
ear
year
tire
here
dear
chair
air
hair

Say and Listen

The spelling words for this lesson contain the /îr/, /âr/, and /īr/ sounds that you hear in *near, care,* and *fire.* Say the spelling words. Listen for the /îr/, /âr/, and /īr/ sounds.

Think and Sort

Look at the letters in each word. Think about how the /îr/, /âr/, or /īr/ sounds are spelled. Spell each word aloud.

1. Write the **seven** /îr/ spelling words. Circle the letters that spell /îr/ in each word.

2. Write the **six** /âr/ spelling words. Circle the letters that spell /âr/ in each word.

3. Write the **three** /īr/ spelling words. Circle the letters that spell /īr/ in each word.

Use the steps on page 6 to study words that are hard for you.

Spelling Patterns

/îr/			/âr/			/īr/
eer	ear	ere	are	air	ere	ire
d**eer**	n**ear**	h**ere**	c**are**	ch**air**	wh**ere**	f**ire**

Spelling and Meaning

Synonyms   Write the spelling word that is a synonym of the underlined word.

1. Look at the long <u>fur</u> on that dog!   _____
2. These <u>steps</u> go to the attic.   _____
3. Don't trip over that <u>cord</u>.   _____
4. The Rileys are <u>loved</u> family friends.   _____

Clues   Write the spelling word for each clue.

5. You breathe this.   _____
6. This animal can have antlers.   _____
7. When you listen, you do this.   _____
8. If you are concerned, you do this.   _____
9. You hear with this.   _____
10. This equals 12 months.   _____
11. This means the opposite of *far.*   _____
12. This is a question word.   _____
13. A car should have a spare one.   _____
14. Matches can start this.   _____
15. This means the opposite of *there.*   _____

Word Story   One spelling word started as the Greek word *cathedra.* *Cathedra* meant "seat." The French changed it to *chaiere.* The English changed it, too. Write the word.

16. _____

Family Tree: *near*   Think about how the *near* words are alike in spelling and meaning. Then add another *near* word to the tree.

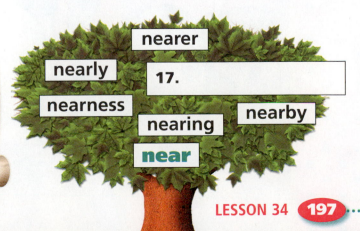

nearer

nearly

17.

nearness

nearing

nearby

near

Use each spelling word once to complete the poem.

A Strange Story

Come sit _____ me, My
         1

_____ children.
      2

Come sit right over _____.
                          3

I have a little story

That I tell just once a _____.
                              4

Put a big log on the _____,
                          5

Come close to my _____.
                        6

And you will hear a story

That will curl all your _____.
                              7

Take _____ to listen closely,
          8

Let me have your _____.
                        9

This is the strangest story

That you may ever _____!
                         10

I was on my way to go to bed,

I was halfway up the stairs,

When a herd of _____ came dancing down,
                        11

Then fourteen polar bears!

Before I could catch a breath of _____ ,
                                                12

Before I could go one step higher,

What do you think went walking by?

A walrus wearing glasses made of _____ .
                                                13

And it was followed by two otters

That rode in an old _____ .
                                14

_____ did those animals come from?
          15

And where did all of them go?

I've asked myself a hundred times,

But still I do not know!

Some nights when it's time for bed,

And I start to climb the _____ ,
                                    16

I think I hear a walrus and otters

And deer and polar bears!

near
care
fire
where
hear
wire
stairs
deer
ear
year
tire
here
dear
chair
air
hair

Write to the Point

Write a poem that tells a story. It can rhyme, but it doesn't have to. The story can be strange or simple. You may want to use one of the lines from "A Strange Story" to start your poem. Try to use spelling words from this lesson.

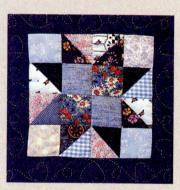

Use the strategies on page 7 when you are not sure how to spell a word.

Proofreading

Proofread the ad for a Cozy Quilt below. Use proofreading marks to correct five spelling mistakes, three capitalization mistakes, and two punctuation mistakes.

Proofreading Marks
- ◯ spell correctly
- ≡ capitalize
- ? add question mark

Cozy Quilt

are you toasty warm on cold winter nights If not, try a Cozy Quilt. do you like to curl up in a chare and read So do I! With a Cozy Quilt, I don't have to sit nere the fire. The aire outside may be cold, but i don't caire. Even on the coldest night of the yeer, my Cozy Quilt keeps me as snug as a bug in a rug!

Dictionary Skills

Pronunciation   Letters and symbols are used to write pronunciations in a dictionary. The letters and symbols can be found in the pronunciation key.

Pronunciation Key

ă	pat	ě	pet	îr	deer	oi	noise	th	thin	ə about,
ā	pay	ē	bee	ŏ	pot	o͝o	took	*th*	this	item, edi-
âr	care	ĭ	pit	ō	toe	o͞o	boot	ŭ	cut	ble, gallop,
ä	father	ī	pie	ô	paw, for	ou	**out**	ûr	**urge**	circus

Write the three words from the boxes that go with each pronunciation.

stairs	wire	where	here	near

fire	year	tire	hair

1. /âr/ _____ _____ _____

2. /īr/ _____ _____ _____

3. /îr/ _____ _____ _____

⭐ Challenge Yourself

Write the Challenge Word for each clue. Check the Spelling Dictionary to see if you are right. Then use separate paper to write sentences showing that you understand the meaning of each Challenge Word.

Challenge Words

careless   dreary

dairy   inspire

4. A beautiful sunset can often do this to an artist. _____

5. Cows are found at this. _____

6. If you do not pay attention to what you do, you are this. _____

7. If a day is dark and cloudy, you can use this word to describe it. _____

Words with -er or -est

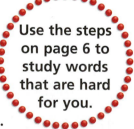

tall, taller, tallest

1. No Change to Base Word

_____

_____

_____

_____

_____

_____

_____

_____

_____

_____

2. Final y Changed to i

_____

_____

_____

_____

3. Final Consonant Doubled

_____

_____

Spelling list:

taller
tallest
longer
longest
dirtier
dirtiest
hotter
hottest
stronger
strongest
greater
greatest
funnier
funniest
sharper
sharpest

Say and Listen

Say each spelling word. Listen for the ending sounds.

Think and Sort

All of the spelling words end in *-er* or *-est*. Spell each word aloud.

Each spelling word is formed by adding *-er* or *-est* to a base word. Look at the letters of each base word.

1. Write the **ten** spelling words that have no change in the base word.

2. Write the **four** spelling words in which the final *y* of the base word is changed to *i*.

3. Write the **two** spelling words in which the final consonant of the base word is doubled.

Use the steps on page 6 to study words that are hard for you.

Spelling Patterns

No Change to Base Word	Final y Changed to i	Final Consonant Doubled
tall**er**		
tall**est**	funn**ier**	hot**ter**
	funn**iest**	hot**test**

Spelling and Meaning

Antonyms   Write the spelling word that is an antonym of the underlined word.

1. Turn on the fan if it gets <u>colder</u>.   _____
2. I need the <u>dullest</u> knife for the steak.   _____
3. An owl's eyes are <u>duller</u> than a robin's.   _____
4. The <u>weakest</u> wrestler is most likely to win.   _____
5. I will put the <u>cleanest</u> clothes in the wash.   _____

Comparisons   Write the spelling word that completes each comparison.

6. An oak tree is _____ than a person.
7. Her joke was the _____ one I ever heard.
8. Mt. Everest is the _____ mountain in the world.
9. Four is _____ than three.
10. A mile is _____ than a foot.
11. An elephant is _____ than a mouse.
12. The Nile River is the _____ river in the world.
13. Summer is usually the _____ season of the year.
14. Who is the _____ basketball player of all time?
15. I thought the joke was _____ than the riddle.

Word Story   Two spelling words come from a word that used to be spelled *dritti*. People began to change its spelling. They made the first *i* change places with the *r*. Then they changed the final *i* to *y*. Write the spelling word that is the *-er* form of the word.

16. _____

Family Tree: *sharper*   *Sharper* is a form of *sharp*. Think about how the *sharp* words are alike in spelling and meaning. Then add another *sharp* word to the tree.

sharpen

sharpest

17.

sharper

sharpener

sharp

Use each spelling word once to complete the story.

Big Splash

Ana, Mara, and Ty were playing in the park. Ana said, "Wow, it's hot today!"

Ty wiped his face and said, "It's _____ than it's been
                                          1
all month."

"It's the _____ it's ever been," cried Mara. She gave
              2
a sharp whistle. Ana gave an even _____ one. But both
                                           3
girls had to cover their ears. Ty's whistle was the _____
                                                        4
of all.

"Oh, Ty. You think you're so great," said Mara.

"You think you're _____ than anyone," cried Ana.
                        5

"Well, my whistle was the _____," boasted Ty. "But
                                6
let's have a real contest. Let's play tug-of-war."

Each one wanted to win. Mara was strong. But Ty thought he
was _____ than Mara. And Ana thought she was the
       7
_____. You don't have to be tall to be strong. Ana
     8
wasn't very tall. Mara was _____ than she was. And Ty
                                 9
was the _____.
            10

"Let's put this mud puddle between us," said Ty. "The loser will
fall and get dirty."

"I'll bet you'll get _____ than I will," said Mara.
                          11

"You'll be the _____ of all," cried Ana.
                    12

Ty and Mara were first. They pulled the rope for a long time. Mara and Ana were next. They pulled for an even _____ time. Ty and Ana were the last to play.
13

Their tug-of-war contest was the _____.
14

Finally Ana pulled Ty into the mud. He fell with a big splash. The mud flew. There were big spots on Ana's face. Mara had mud on her sweater.

"You may be the winner, Ana, but you sure look funny," said Mara.

"No _____ than you," said Ana.
15

Ty just sat in the puddle grinning. "And I'll bet I look the _____ of all!" he laughed.
16

taller
tallest
longer
longest
dirtier
dirtiest
hotter
hottest
stronger
strongest
greater
greatest
funnier
funniest
sharper
sharpest

Spelling and Writing

taller
tallest
longer
longest
dirtier
dirtiest
hotter
hottest
stronger
strongest
greater
greatest
funnier
funniest
sharper
sharpest

Write to the Point

In "Big Splash" Ana, Mara, and Ty had a contest. Think of a contest you would like to have. Make a sign announcing the contest. Tell where and when it will be held and what the prize will be. Try to use spelling words from this lesson in your sign.

Use the strategies on page 7 when you are not sure how to spell a word.

Proofreading

Proofread this paragraph from a newspaper article. Use proofreading marks to correct five spelling mistakes, three capitalization mistakes, and two punctuation mistakes.

Proofreading Marks
◯ spell correctly
≡ capitalize
⊙ add period

Gabby's Garden Tips

spring is the greatist season of them all The sun shines stronger than in winter. The days are longger. the trees and grass grow taler and faster. Early spring is the time to start a flower garden Digging in the earth might make your hands dirtyer than watching TV, but it will also make you happier! A flower garden is something everyone can enjoy. having lots of bright, colorful flowers will make your spring even grater !

Language Connection

Adjectives   An adjective describes a noun or pronoun. It tells which, what kind, or how many.

> The **strong** man lifted the box.   Mike is **strong**.

Add *-er* to most adjectives to compare two people or things.
Add *-est* to compare more than two people or things.

> Cliff is **stronger** than Mike.   Paul is the **strongest** of all.

Use the correct word from the boxes to write each sentence.

greater   hotter   funniest   tallest

1. Sharon tells the ___ jokes we've ever heard.

_____

2. The sun is ___ today than it was yesterday.

_____

3. Gigi is the ___ girl on the basketball team.

_____

4. Twenty is ___ than ten.

_____

Challenge Yourself

What do you think each Challenge Word means? Check the Spelling Dictionary to see if you are right. Then use separate paper to write sentences showing that you understand the meaning of each Challenge Word.

Challenge Words	
weirder	weirdest
shakier	shakiest

5. Which is **weirder** —blue hair or a green face?

6. The shadows made the **weirdest** shapes on the wall.

7. The chair with the short leg is **shakier** than the other.

8. My chair is the **shakiest** of all.

Unit 6 Review
Lessons 31–35

Use the steps on page 6 to study words that are hard for you.

31

strong
talk
bought
because
draw

Words with /ô/

Unscramble the letters in parentheses. Then write the spelling word to complete the sentence.

1. (thobug) Maria _____ two tickets to the concert.

2. (abesceu) We could not see _____ of the tall post.

3. (torsgn) That horse has very _____ legs.

4. (kalt) Let's _____ about the game.

5. (ward) Can you _____ a picture of the house?

32

autumn
before
floor
pour
quart

More Words with /ô/

Write the spelling word for each clue.

6. This is a measure for liquids. _____

7. You do this with water in a pitcher. _____

8. This season comes before winter. _____

9. This word is the opposite of *after*. _____

10. This can be covered with tile or carpet. _____

33

count
hour
tower
owl

Words with /ou/

Write the spelling word that completes each analogy.

11. *Days* is to *week* as *minutes* is to _____.

12. *Terrier* is to *dog* as _____ is to *bird*.

13. *Read* is to *book* as _____ is to *money*.

14. *House* is to *garage* as *castle* is to _____.

34

deer
near
here
care
air
where
wire

Words with /îr/, /âr/, or /īr/

Write the spelling word that completes each sentence.

15. The smell of lilacs filled the _____.

16. The _____ darted across the road.

17. Do you know _____ my keys are?

18. We can rest _____ in the shade.

19. The cage was made of wood and _____.

20. Our hotel is _____ the park.

21. Heidi takes good _____ of her pet.

35

greater
sharpest
funnier
hottest

Words with -er or -est

Write the spelling word that belongs in each group.

22. sharp   sharper   _____

23. great   _____   greatest

24. hot   hotter   _____

25. funny   _____   funniest

26. /ô/ Words

27. /ou/ Words

28. /îr/ Words

29. /âr/ Words

30. /īr/ Word

Review Sort

pour	floor	before	deer
care	strong	hour	bought
where	here	near	air
autumn	draw	quart	count
talk	tower	owl	wire

26. Write the **nine** /ô/ words.

27. Write the **four** /ou/ words.

28. Write the **three** /îr/ words.

29. Write the **three** /âr/ words.

30. Write the **one** /īr/ word.

These four words have been sorted into two groups. Explain how the words in each group are alike and how they are different.

31. greater   funnier

32. sharpest   hottest

Writer's Workshop

A Narrative

A narrative that continues another story is called a sequel. A sequel is a whole story with a beginning, middle, and an end. It usually has the same characters and setting as the original story. Here is part of Julio's sequel to "The Frog Prince" on pages 180 and 181.

Libby Returns

Libby could not forget about the frog, so the next time she was in the mall, she went to the pet shop. She looked for the frog, but it was not there. When she saw Mr. Muller, she asked, "Where has the frog gone?"

Prewriting   To write his narrative, Julio followed the steps in the writing process. After he thought about his sequel, he completed a story map. The story map helped him decide what would happen at the beginning, middle, and end of his sequel. Julio's story map is shown here. Study what he did.

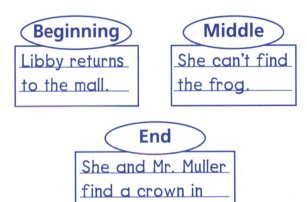

Beginning
Libby returns to the mall.

Middle
She can't find the frog.

End
She and Mr. Muller find a crown in the pond.

It's Your Turn!

Write your own sequel to a story. Choose any story that you have read or heard before. After you have chosen a story to continue, make a story map. Then follow the other steps in the writing process — writing, revising, proofreading, and publishing. Try to use spelling words from this lesson in your sequel.

Commonly Misspelled Words

about	family	name	that's
above	favorite	nice	their
across	finally	now	then
again	friend	once	there
a lot	friends	one	they
always	from	our	though
another	get	out	today
baby	getting	outside	too
because	girl	party	two
been	goes	people	upon
before	guess	play	very
beginning	have	please	want
bought	hear	pretty	was
boy	her	read	went
buy	here	really	were
can	him	right	when
came	his	said	where
children	house	saw	white
color	into	scared	with
come	know	school	would
cousin	like	sent	write
didn't	little	some	writing
does	made	store	wrote
don't	make	swimming	your
every	many	teacher	you're

Spelling Table

Sound	Spellings	Examples
/ă/	a a_e ai au	ask, have, plaid, laugh
/ā/	a a_e ai ay ea eigh ey	table, save, rain, gray, break, eight, they
/ä/	a ea	father, heart
/âr/	air are ere	chair, care, where
/b/	b bb	best, rabbit
/ch/	ch tch	child, catch
/d/	d dd	dish, add
/ĕ/	e ea ie ue a ai ay	best, read, friend, guess, many, said, says
/ē/	e e_e ea ee ei eo ey y	even, these, each, meet, receive, people, key, city
/f/	f ff gh	fly, off, laugh
/g/	g gg	go, egg
/h/	h wh	hot, who
/ĭ/	i ui e ee u a	inside, build, pretty, been, busy, luggage
/ī/	i i_e ie igh eye uy y	tiny, drive, pie, high, eyes, buy, fly
/îr/	ear eer eir ere	year, deer, weird, here
/j/	j g	jog, danger
/k/	k c ck ch	keep, coat, kick, school
/ks/	x	six
/kw/	qu	quiet
/l/	l ll	late, tell
/m/	m mb mm	much, comb, hammer
/n/	n kn nn	need, know, beginning
/ng/	n ng	thank, bring

Sound	Spellings	Examples
/ŏ/	o a	shop, was
/ō/	o o_e oa oe ou ow	both, hole, road, toe, boulder, slow
/oi/	oi oy	point, enjoy
/ô/	o oa oo ou ough a au aw	off, coarse, door, four, brought, tall, autumn, draw
/o͝o/	oo ou u u_e	book, could, pull, sure
/o͞o/	oo ou u_e ue ew o	noon, you, June, blue, news, two
/ou/	ou ow	about, owl
/p/	p pp	place, dropped
/r/	r rr wr	rain, sorry, write
/s/	s ss c	safe, dress, city
/sh/	sh s	shook, sure
/t/	t tt ed	take, matter, thanked
/th/	th	then
/th/	th	third
/ŭ/	u o oe	such, mother, does
/ûr/	ur ir er or ear ere our	curl, girl, dessert, world, learn, were, flourish
/v/	v f	even, of
/w/	w wh o	walk, when, one
/y/	y	year
/yo͞o/	u_e ew ue	use, few, Tuesday
/z/	z zz s	sneeze, blizzard, says
/ə/	a e i o u	along, misery, estimate, lion, subtract

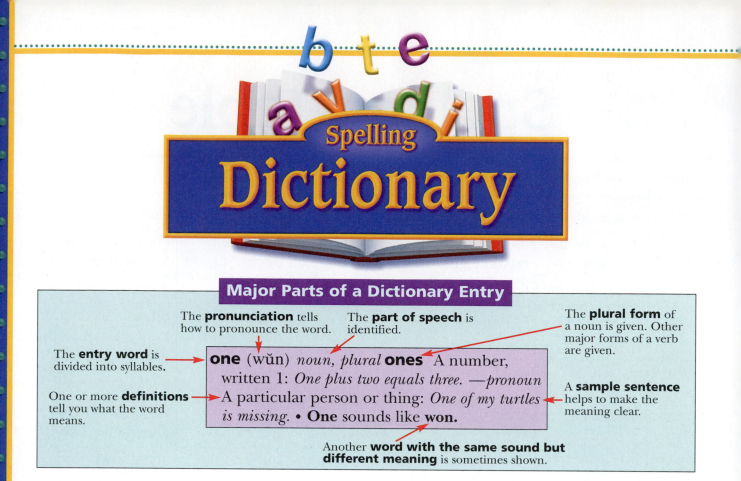

Spelling Dictionary

Major Parts of a Dictionary Entry

The **pronunciation** tells how to pronounce the word.

The **part of speech** is identified.

The **plural form** of a noun is given. Other major forms of a verb are given.

The **entry word** is divided into syllables.

One or more **definitions** tell you what the word means.

one (wŭn) *noun, plural* **ones** A number, written 1: *One plus two equals three.* —*pronoun* A particular person or thing: *One of my turtles is missing.* • **One** sounds like **won.**

A **sample sentence** helps to make the meaning clear.

Another **word with the same sound but different meaning** is sometimes shown.

---

able | ago

a·ble (ā′ bəl) *adjective* **abler, ablest** Having enough skill to do something; capable: *Arnold, the circus elephant, is able to stand on his head.*

a·bout (ə bout′) *preposition* Of; concerning: *Do you know the story about Goldilocks and the three bears?* —*adverb* Almost; nearly: *This glass is about empty.*

add (ăd) *verb* **added, adding** To find the sum of: *When we add 2 and 6, we get a total of 8.*

ad·dress (ə drĕs′) *or* (ăd′ rĕs′) *noun, plural* **addresses** The place where a person lives or receives mail: *I want to mail a birthday card to Nina, but I don't know her address.*

ad·mire (ăd mīr′) *verb* **admired, admiring 1.** To respect: *I admire your courage.* **2.** To look at or regard with pleasure and appreciation: *Our class admired the drawings of the animals.*

a·do·be (ə dō′ bē) *noun, plural* **adobes 1.** Brick made of straw and clay that is dried in the sun. **2.** A building made out of these bricks: *Her house is made of adobe.*

a·fraid (ə frād′) *adjective* Frightened; full of fear: *I'm not afraid of the dark.*

af·ter (ăf′ tər) *preposition* Following; at a later time than: *I went to Rona's after dinner.*

a·gain (ə gĕn′) *adverb* Once more; another time: *It's time for a spelling test again.*

a·gent (ā′ jənt) *noun, plural* **agents 1.** A person who acts for another person, company, or government: *His father is an insurance agent.* **2.** Something that produces or causes a certain effect: *Too much rain is the agent of a flood.*

a·go (ə gō′) *adverb* Past; before the time it is now: *The bus left five minutes ago.*

ag•o•ny (ăg′ ə nē) *noun, plural* **agonies** Great pain or suffering: *I broke my leg and was in agony.*

aid (ād) *verb* **aided, aiding** To help or assist: *Carla will aid you in finding a seat.*

aim (ām) *verb* **aimed, aiming 1.** To point at something: *Aim the dart at the target.* **2.** To have a goal or purpose: *We aim to please our teacher.*

air (âr) *noun* **1.** The mixture of gases surrounding the earth: *I like the cool air.* **2.** The space above the earth: *The air was full of kites.*

a•like (ə līk′) *adjective* Similar; like one another: *The goldfish in my fish tank are all alike.*

al•most (ôl′ mōst′) *or* (ôl mōst′) *adverb* Nearly: *It is almost time for lunch.*

a•lone (ə lōn′) *adverb* By oneself: *I like to walk by the sea all alone.*

a•long (ə lông′) *or* (ə lŏng′) *preposition* Beside the length of: *We walked along the beach.* —*adverb* Together; with someone: *When Calvin goes for a walk, his dog goes along.*

al•ways (ôl′ wāz) *or* (ôl′ wĭz) *adverb* At all times; every time: *Sonya always reads before she goes to bed.*

a•pol•o•gize (ə pŏl′ ə jīz′) *verb* **apologized, apologizing** To say one is sorry: *I apologize for being late to class.*

ap•ple (ăp′ əl) *noun, plural* **apples** A round fruit that is red, yellow, or green: *My favorite kind of fruit pie is apple.*

A•pril (ā′ prəl) *noun* The fourth month of the year: *April is a spring month.*

arc•tic (ärk′ tĭk) *or* (är′ tĭk) *adjective* Very cold: *The arctic air froze the water in the lake.*

aren't (ärnt) *or* (är′ ənt) The contraction of "are not": *Why aren't you coming to the playground with us?*

arm (ärm) *noun, plural* **arms** The part of the body between the hand and the shoulder: *Zelda's arm hurt from pitching.*

a•round (ə round′) *adverb* In a circle: *I saw the bird fly around.* —*preposition* About; here and there: *I travel around the country.*

art (ärt) *noun, plural* **arts 1.** A painting, drawing, or sculpture. **2.** A skill or craft: *Dancing is an art.*

ar•tis•tic (är tĭs′ tĭk) *adjective* **1.** Having to do with art or artists: *He has artistic interests.* **2.** Showing talent, skill, or good taste.

ask (ăsk) *verb* **asked, asking 1.** To put a question to: *I asked my father where he was born.* **2.** To request: *I asked for a small pizza.*

as•sure (ə shŏŏr′) *verb* **assured, assuring 1.** To make sure or certain. **2.** To make less afraid: *Do you assure me that the dog will not bite?*

ate Look up **eat.** • **Ate** sounds like **eight.**

ath•let•ic (ăth lĕt′ ĭk) *adjective* **1.** Strong and active: *The athletic girl won every race.* **2.** Having to do with or for sports or athletes.

at•tempt (ə tĕmpt′) *noun, plural* **attempts** A try or effort: *I made an attempt to draw a picture of my cat.*

Au•gust (ô′ gəst) *noun* The eighth month of the year: *The weather is hot here in August.*

au•tumn (ô′ təm) *noun, plural* **autumns** The season of the year coming between summer and winter; fall: *Every autumn the leaves change color and then fall off the trees.*

215

a•way (ə wā′) *adverb* **1.** In a different direction or place: *James is away from school.* **2.** From a place: *Take the dogs away.*

bar•be•cue (bär′ bĭ kyōō′) *noun, plural* **barbecues** A meal cooked outdoors over an open fire: *I like to eat barbecue.* —*verb* **barbecued, barbecuing** To cook over an open fire outdoors: *We will barbecue the meat.*

bark¹ (bärk) *noun, plural* **barks** The sharp, explosive sound made by a dog or fox: *I could hear my dog's bark.* —*verb* **barked, bark•ing** To make the sharp sound a dog makes: *Fido likes to bark at cats.*

bark² (bärk) *noun, plural* **barks** The outer covering of trees and other woody plants: *The bark of a birch tree is thin.*

barn (bärn) *noun, plural* **barns** A farm building used for storing grain and hay and for keeping livestock: *The horses ran into the barn.*

be (bē) *verb* **am, is, was** (wŏz) *or* (wŭz) *or* (wəz), **were** (wûr), **been** (bĭn), **being** **1.** To equal in identity or meaning: *That girl is my sister.* **2.** To have or show a certain quality or characteristic: *I am tall and thin.* **3.** To belong to a certain group or class: *Whales are mammals.* **4.** To occupy a certain place or position: *Your books have been here since yesterday.* **5.** To live; to exist: *Once upon a time, there were three bears.* **6.** To take place; to happen: *Thanksgiving is next week.* —*helping verb* (used with other verbs): *I am teaching my dog a new trick.*

bear (bâr) *verb* **bore, born** (bôrn), **bearing** **1.** To give birth to: *Some snakes lay eggs, and some bear their young.* **2.** To come into being: *George Washington was born on February 22, 1732.*
• **Bear** sounds like **bare.**

be•cause (bĭ kôz′) *or* (bĭ kŭz′) *conjunction* Since; for the reason that: *The class laughed because the cartoons were so silly.*

been Look up **be.**

be•fore (bĭ fôr′) *conjunction* Earlier than; ahead of: *Liz did her chores before lunch.*

be•gin (bĭ gĭn′) *verb* **began, begun, beginning** (bĭ gĭn′ ĭng) To start: *The teams were ready to begin the game.*

be•gin•ning (bĭ gĭn′ ĭng) *noun, plural* **beginnings** The first part: *At the beginning of the race, Carlos was ahead.*

be•hind (bĭ hīnd′) *preposition* **1.** Following: *Ling and Trina were walking behind Jeff.* **2.** At the back of: *Maria hid behind a tree.*

be•long (bĭ lông′) *or* (bĭ lŏng′) *verb* **belonged, belonging** To be owned by: *These pencils belong to me.*

best (bĕst) *adjective* Most excellent, finest: *It was the best ice cream she had ever eaten.* Look up **good, well.**

bet•ter (bĕt′ ər) *adjective* More excellent than another: *We have a better band than any other school.* Look up **good, well.**

bird (bûrd) *noun, plural* **birds** An animal with wings and feathers that lays eggs: *A cardinal is a bird with bright red feathers.*

black (blăk) *noun* The darkest color; the color of coal: *Black is the color of crows.* —*adjective* **blacker, blackest** Having this color: *Mom wore a black dress.*

blend (blĕnd) *verb* **blended, blending** To put together; mix: *Blend the eggs and sugar.* —*noun, plural* **blends** Something that has been mixed.

block (blŏk) *noun, plural* **blocks** Part of a city, often a square, with streets on all sides: *I live one block away.* —*verb* **blocked, blocking** To get in the way of: *The cow blocked the railroad track.*

blow (blō) *verb* **blew, blown, blowing** To be in motion, as the air: *Hold onto your hat, or the wind will blow it away.*

blue (blŌŌ) *adjective* **bluer, bluest**
Having the color of the clear sky during
the day: *Benjamin wore a blue jacket.*
• **Blue** sounds like **blew.**

boat (bŌt) *noun, plural* **boats** A vessel that
travels on water: *My sister and I went for a
ride on the boat.*

bod•y (bŏd′ ē) *noun, plural* **bodies** All
of a person or animal except the mind:
The human body is very complex.

boil (boil) *verb* **boiled, boiling** To heat
a liquid until bubbles form and steam is
given off: *I boiled some water to make tea.*

book (bŏŏk) *noun, plural* **books** Printed
sheets of paper held together between two
covers: *Richie went to the library to get a book.*

born Look up **bear.**

both (bŌth) *pronoun* The one as well as the
other: *Both of them can play the French horn.*
—*conjunction* (used with *and*): *Both Mom
and Dad were at work.*

bot•tle (bŏt′ l) *noun, plural* **bottles** A
hollow container made of glass or plastic
that can be closed with a cap: *The children
drank juice from the bottles.*

bot•tom (bŏt′ əm) *noun, plural* **bottoms**
The lowest part of anything: *I saw my dad
at the bottom of the hill.*

bough (bou) *noun, plural* **boughs** A large
or main branch of a tree: *The nest is on the
bough of the tree.*

bought Look up **buy.**

boy (boi) *noun, plural* **boys** A male child:
My dog chased the boy on the bike.

break (brāk) *verb* **broke, broken,
breaking** **1.** To crack or damage; to
come apart: *Did you break the dish when you
dropped it?* **2.** To crack the bone of: *Rosa
fell off her bike and broke her arm.*

bring (brĭng) *verb* **brought** (brôt),
bringing To carry or take something to
a place or person: *He brought his photo
album to school.*

Pronunciation Key

ă	pat	îr	deer	*th*	**th**is
ā	pay	ŏ	pot	ŭ	cut
âr	care	ō	toe	ûr	urge
ä	father	ô	paw, for	ə	about,
ĕ	pet	oi	noise		item,
ē	bee	ŏŏ	took		edible,
ĭ	pit	ōō	boot		gallop,
ī	pie	ou	out		circus
		th	thin		

broil (broil) *verb* **broiled, broiling** To
cook by holding directly over or under
heat: *Mia broiled the steaks for dinner.*

broth (brôth) *or* (brŏth) *noun, plural*
broths A thin clear soup made from the
water in which meat, fish, or vegetables have
been boiled: *We had chicken broth for lunch.*

brought Look up **bring.**

brown (broun) *adjective* **browner,
brownest** Having the color of coffee or
chocolate: *The dead leaves were brown.*

build (bĭld) *verb* **built, building** To make
something by putting materials or parts
together: *Many birds build nests in the spring.*

bu•reau (byŏŏr′ ō) *noun, plural* **bureaus**
A chest of drawers: *Put it on the bureau.*

bus•y (bĭz′ ē) *adjective* **busier, busiest**
At work; active: *She is busy doing her homework.*

but•ter (bŭt′ ər) *noun* A soft, yellow fat
made from cream: *I like butter on corn.*

buy (bī) *verb* **bought** (bôt), **buying** To
get by paying a price: *He bought a model
rocket at the hobby shop.* • **Buy** sounds like **by.**

buz•zard (bŭz′ ərd) *noun, plural*
buzzards A very large bird
with a sharp, hooked beak
and long, sharp claws; a
vulture: *The buzzard was
in the tree.*

by (bī) *preposition* Beside or
near: *Leave your boots by the door.*
• **By** sounds like **buy.**

ca•ble (kā′ bəl) *noun, plural* **cables**
A strong, thick rope often made of steel
wire: *The boat is held to the dock by a cable.*

came Look up **come.**

can (kăn) *or* (kən) *helping verb* **could**
(kŏŏd) To be able to: *We could see that
the man was angry.*

can't (kănt) The contraction of "cannot":
I can't see any stars tonight.

card (kärd) *noun, plural* **cards** A small
rectangular piece of cardboard or plastic:
I sent my pen pal a birthday card.

care (kâr) *noun, plural* **cares** Close
attention: *The painter picked her colors with care.*
—*verb* **cared, caring** To be concerned:
Millie cared what people thought about her.

care•less (kâr′ lĭs) *adjective* Not paying
attention to what one is doing: *I fell off
my bike because I was careless.*

car•ry (kăr′ ē) *verb* **carries, carried,
carrying** To take from one place to
another: *Will you help me carry this box?*

car•ton (kär′ tn) *noun, plural* **cartons**
A container or box made of cardboard,
paper, plastic, or other materials and used
for holding liquids or other objects: *We will
recycle the egg carton.*

ca•su•al (kăzh′ ōō əl) *adjective* Right for
informal wear: *Sam wears casual clothes.*

catch (kăch) *or* (kĕch) *verb* **caught,
catching** **1.** To get hold of; capture: *Billy
tried to catch the cat.* **2.** To reach or get to
in time: *I had to hurry to catch the train.*

cav•ern (kăv′ ərn) *noun, plural* **caverns**
A large cave: *Raul likes to explore caverns.*

cel•e•bra•tion (sĕl′ ə brā′ shən) *noun,
plural* **celebrations** A party or other
activity carried on to honor a special
occasion: *We had a celebration the last
day of school.*

cem•e•ter•y (sĕm′ ĭ tĕr′ ē) *noun, plural*
cemeteries A place where dead people
are buried: *The class put flowers on the
graves in the cemetery.*

cent (sĕnt) *noun, plural* **cents** A coin that is
1/100 of a dollar; a penny: *Carlos bought the
notebook for 99 cents.* • **Cent** sounds like **sent.**

chair (châr) *noun, plural* **chairs** A seat for
one person, usually having four legs and a
back: *The chair was soft and comfortable.*

change (chānj) *verb* **changed, changing**
1. To make different: *Leaves change color in
the fall.* **2.** To replace; exchange: *I'll change
this dress for a different one.* —*noun, plural*
changes A thing that has become
different: *We all noticed the change in
her hair.*

child (chīld) *noun, plural* **children**
(**chĭl′** drən) A young boy or girl: *Every
child in the school went on the picnic. All
children like fairy tales.*

chil•dren Look up **child.**

chime (chīm) *noun,
plural* **chimes**
1. A set of bells or
pipes that make
musical sounds.
2. A musical sound
made by bells or a similar
sound: *The chime of the doorbell woke me.*

choice (chois) *noun, plural* **choices** The
power or chance to choose: *They had their
choice of peanut butter sandwiches or tuna
salad for lunch.*

cir•cu•lar (sûr′ kyə lər) *adjective* Shaped
like a circle; round: *The circular drawing
was well done.*

cit•y (sĭt′ ē) *noun, plural* **cities** A large
or important town: *Mom goes to the city every
day to work.*

clank (klăngk) *verb* **clanked, clanking**
To make a sound like two pieces of metal
hitting each other: *The hammer clanked
against the iron bell.*

class (klăs) *noun, plural* **classes** A group of students taught by the same teacher or group of teachers: *Our class took a trip to the museum.*

clock (klŏk) *noun, plural* **clocks** An instrument that tells time: *According to the kitchen clock, I was late again.*

close (klōs) *adjective* **closer, closest** Near: *He is standing close to the door.* —*verb* (klōz) **closed, closing** To shut: *He closed the heavy suitcase.*

clown (kloun) *noun, plural* **clowns** A person who has a job in the circus or on stage making people laugh: *The clowns looked so funny.*

coarse (kôrs) *adjective* **coarser, coarsest** **1.** Made of large bits: *The sand on the beach was coarse.* **2.** Rough: *Coarse wool makes me itch.*

coat (kōt) *noun, plural* **coats** A piece of clothing worn over other clothes to keep warm: *Keesha's new coat was too big.*

coax (kōks) *verb* **coaxed, coaxing** To try to persuade or convince by mild urging: *Mom had to coax me into going.*

co•coa (kō′ kō′) *noun* A drink made with chocolate, sugar, and milk or water: *We drink hot cocoa in winter.*

coin (koin) *noun, plural* **coins** A piece of round, flat metal stamped by the government, used for money: *I had a lot of coins in my pocket.*

comb (kōm) *noun, plural* **combs** A thin piece of hard material with teeth, used to arrange hair: *While Selena was untangling her hair, the comb broke.* —*verb* **combed, combing** **1.** To arrange the hair. **2.** To look thoroughly: *I combed the house for my missing ring.*

come (kŭm) *verb* **came** (kām), **coming** **1.** To draw near; approach: *The lion came closer and closer to the mouse.* **2.** To be available: *The toy robot came with two batteries.*

Pronunciation Key

ă	pat	îr	deer	*th*	this
ā	pay	ŏ	pot	ŭ	cut
âr	care	ō	toe	ûr	urge
ä	father	ô	paw, for	ə	about,
ĕ	pet	oi	noise		item,
ē	bee	ŏŏ	took		edible,
ĭ	pit	ōō	boot		gallop,
ī	pie	ou	out		circus
		th	thin		

com•ment (kŏm′ ĕnt′) *noun, plural* **comments** A remark or note that explains something or gives an opinion: *James made a comment about the news.*

con•sent (kən sĕnt′) *verb* **consented, consenting** To agree to; to give permission: *Michael consented to cleaning his room once a week.*

con•sole (kən sōl′) *verb* **consoled, consoling** To comfort: *When Kim's pet died, Belinda consoled her.*

con•tain (kən tān′) *verb* **contained, containing** To have in it; hold: *The bowl contains soup.*

cook (kŏŏk) *verb* **cooked, cooking** To prepare food for eating by using heat: *Cook the rice until it is fluffy.*

cook•ie (kŏŏk′ ē) *noun, plural* **cookies** A small, flat, sweet cake: *The cookies were shaped like hearts.*

cor•ner (kôr′ nər) *noun, plural* **corners** The place where two lines or sides meet: *My dog ate a corner of my homework paper.*

cor•ri•dor (kôr′ ĭ dər) *or* (kŏr′ ĭ dər) *noun, plural* **corridors** A long hall or passage in a building: *The corridor in the hotel was wide.*

could Look up **can.**

could•n't (kŏŏd′ nt) The contraction of "could not": *We couldn't go to the beach.*

could•'ve (kŏŏd′ əv) The contraction of "could have": *Lisa could've gone to the zoo, but she was sick.*

219

count (kount) *noun, plural* **counts**
The number reached by counting: *A count showed that one marble was missing.* —*verb* **counted, counting** To say numbers in order: *Ty's baby sister can count to 20.*

cov•er (kŭv′ ər) *verb* **covered, covering**
To put or lay over: *I covered my bread with peanut butter.* —*noun, plural* **covers**
Something that is put over another thing: *He hid the present under the covers on his bed.*

crin•kle (krĭng′ kəl) *verb* **crinkled, crinkling** To wrinkle; crumple: *Betsy tried not to crinkle the wrapping paper.*

cry (krī) *verb* **cries, cried, crying**
1. To weep; shed tears: *Some people cry when they are happy.* **2.** To shout or call loudly: *If I need help, I'll cry out.*

curl (kûrl) *verb* **curled, curling** To twist into curves or coils: *The snake curled around the rock.* —*noun, plural* **curls** A coil of hair; a ringlet: *She wore her hair in curls.*

cy•cle (sī′ kəl) *noun, plural* **cycles**
1. A bicycle, tricycle, or motorcycle: *My cycle is broken.* **2.** A series of events that happen over and over in the same order: *People enjoy the cycle of seasons.*

dair•y (dâr′ ē) *noun, plural* **dairies**
A farm where cows are raised to produce milk: *Our class took a field trip to the dairy.*

dan•ger (dān′ jər) *noun, plural* **dangers**
The chance that something harmful might happen: *A police officer faces danger every day.*

dark (därk) *adjective* **darker, darkest**
Having little or no light: *The cave was very dark inside.* —*noun* Nightfall: *The street lights come on after dark.*

daw•dle (dôd′ l) *verb* **dawdled, dawdling** To take more time than necessary: *I often dawdle on my way home from school.*

dear (dîr) *adjective* **dearer, dearest**
Loved: *Billy is a dear friend of mine.*
• **Dear** sounds like **deer.**

de•bate (dĭ bāt′) *verb* **debated, debating 1.** To think about in order to decide: *I debated which book to buy.*
2. To discuss or argue reasons for and against something.

de•ceive (dĭ sēv′) *verb* **deceived, deceiving** To make a person believe something that is not true; mislead: *It was wrong to deceive my parents.*

De•cem•ber (dĭ sĕm′ bər) *noun* The twelfth month of the year: *We are going skiing in December.*

deer (dîr) *noun, plural* **deer** A hoofed animal that can run very fast: *Look at the beautiful antlers on that male deer.*
• **Deer** sounds like **dear.**

de•fine (dĭ fīn′) *verb* **defined, defining**
To give or explain the meaning of: *Our teacher told us to define the spelling words.*

de•pos•it (dĭ pŏz′ ĭt) *verb* **deposited, depositing 1.** To put or place; set down: *I deposited my toys in the box.* **2.** To put money in the bank.

de•sign•er (dĭ zī′ nər) *noun, plural* **designers** A person who makes the plan, pattern, or drawing for something: *The designer told us about her idea for a new doll.*

des•sert (dĭ zûrt′) *noun, plural* **desserts** Food served last at a meal: *We had dessert after we finished dinner.*

de•vour (dĭ vour′) *verb* **devoured, devouring** To eat in a hungry way: *The child will devour her lunch.*

did•n't (dĭd′ nt) The contraction of "did not": *I didn't know who you were.*

dirt (dûrt) *noun* Loose earth or soil: *He drew a map in the dirt with a stick.*

dirt•y (dûr′ tē) *adjective* **dirtier, dirtiest**
Not clean: *Amy's shoes were dirtier than mine.
Eric's were the dirtiest.*

dish (dĭsh) *noun, plural* **dishes 1.** A plate
or bowl used for holding food: *The clown
balanced a dish on his nose.* **2.** A particular
food: *Barbara's favorite dish was spaghetti.*

dis•may (dĭs mā′) *noun* A feeling of fear
or loss of courage when danger or trouble
comes: *I felt dismay when my rabbit got out
of its pen.*

dis•pute (dĭ spyo͞ot′) *noun, plural*
disputes An argument or quarrel:
My friend and I had a dispute.

do (do͞o) *verb* **does** (duz), **did, done**
(dun), **doing 1.** To perform; complete:
*Bibi, the circus monkey, is always doing
things that make people laugh.* **2.** To be
good enough: *No one had done as well on
the test as Valerie.* —*helping verb* (used to
ask questions): *Does she swim?*

does Look up **do.**

does•n't (dŭz′ nt) The contraction of
"does not": *She doesn't want to play the
game anymore.*

dome (dōm) *noun, plural*
domes A round roof or
top that looks like half of
a ball: *The building had a
dome at the top.*

done Look up **do.**

don't (dōnt) The contraction of "do not":
Don't sit on that wet bench.

door (dôr) *noun, plural* **doors 1.** A
movable panel that swings or slides to open
or close the entrance to a room, building, or
vehicle: *Raquel slammed the door behind her.*
2. A doorway: *Marta walked through the door.*

doubt•ful (dout′ fəl) *adjective* Feeling,
showing, or causing uncertainty; not sure:
Kim was doubtful that she could stay awake.

down¹ (doun) *adverb* From a higher to a
lower point on: *The ball rolled down the hill.*

Pronunciation Key

ă	pat	îr	deer	*th*	this
ā	pay	ŏ	pot	ŭ	cut
âr	care	ō	toe	ûr	urge
ä	father	ô	paw, for	ə	about,
ĕ	pet	oi	noise		item,
ē	bee	o͝o	took		edible,
ĭ	pit	o͞o	boot		gallop,
ī	pie	ou	out		circus
		th	thin		

down² (doun) *noun* The soft under
feathers of birds: *The bird had soft down.*

draw (drô) *verb* **drew, drawn, drawing**
To make a picture with pen, pencil, crayon,
etc.: *I can draw great pictures of airplanes.*

dream (drēm) *noun, plural* **dreams**
Something felt, thought, or seen during
sleep: *I had a dream about a giant bee.*
—*verb* **dreamed** or **dreamt, dreaming**
To think, feel, or see during sleep; to have
dreams: *Amy dreamed that she could fly.*

drea•ry (drîr′ ē) *adjective* **drearier,
dreariest** Sad; gloomy: *The rainy day
was dreary.*

dress (drĕs) *noun, plural* **dresses** A piece
of clothing worn by women and girls, usually
having a top and skirt made in one piece:
Ella bought a new dress for the class party.
—*verb* **dressed, dressing** To put
clothes on: *Get dressed and we'll go shopping.*

drive (drīv) *verb* **drove, driven, driving
1.** To steer a vehicle: *Drive the car carefully.*
2. To carry in a vehicle: *My mom promised to
drive me to the rodeo.* —*noun, plural* **drives**
A ride in a vehicle: *Let's go for a drive.*

drop (drŏp) *verb* **dropped, dropping**
To fall or let fall: *I dropped the glass.*

each (ēch) *adjective* Every one of: *Each
student in the class gave me a report.*

ear (îr) *noun, plural* **ears** **1.** The part of the body with which animals and people hear: *An elephant's ears are big and floppy.* **2.** Attention: *This message is important, so give me your ear.*

earth (ûrth) *noun* **1.** The planet on which human beings live: *The earth is the third planet from the sun.* **2.** Soil; ground: *We planted a tree in the earth.*

eat (ēt) *verb* **ate** (āt), **eaten, eating** To take meals: *I ate dinner at home.*

egg (ĕg) *noun, plural* **eggs** The contents of a chicken egg, used as food: *I like to crack the shells of eggs.*

eight (āt) *noun* The number that follows seven: *Four plus four is eight.* —*adjective* Being one more than seven in number: *An octopus has eight tentacles.* • **Eight** sounds like **ate.**

end (ĕnd) *noun, plural* **ends** The finish of a thing: *The road comes to an end at the river.* —*verb* **ended, ending** To finish; to bring to an end: *The concert ended with a fireworks show.*

end•ing (ĕn' dĭng) *noun, plural* **endings** The last part: *The movie had a scary ending.*

en•dure (ĕn dŏŏr') *or* (ĕn dyŏŏr') *verb* **endured, enduring** **1.** To put up with: *The campers had to endure cold weather.* **2.** To continue; last. *The pyramids have endured a long time.*

en•joy (ĕn joi') *verb* **enjoyed, enjoying** To like to do: *I enjoy singing along with her.*

en•joy•ment (ĕn joi' mənt) *noun, plural* **enjoyments** Joy; pleasure: *We get enjoyment from a good book.*

es•ti•mate (ĕs' tə māt') *verb* **estimated, estimating** To guess by thinking about clearly: *We estimated that the trip would take five hours.*

e•ven (ē' vən) *adjective* Smooth; flat: *Willy likes to ride his bike on this road because it's so even.* —*adverb* **1.** Although it seems unlikely: *The boys were all dressed up, even Coby.*

eve•ry (ĕv' rē) *adjective* All in an entire group; each one: *Mr. Lee read every mystery book in the library.*

eye (ī) *noun, plural* **eyes** **1.** One of two round organs with which a person or animal sees: *My eyes followed the home run right out of the field.* **2.** A close watch: *Please keep an eye on my bike.*

fa•ble (fā' bəl) *noun, plural* **fables** A story that teaches a lesson: *My favorite fable is about the lion and the mouse.*

face (fās) *noun, plural* **faces** The front of the head: *Raymond had spots on his face from the measles.*

fal•ter (fôl' tər) *verb* **faltered, faltering** To act, speak, or move in an unsteady way: *My voice was faltering when I gave my speech.*

fam•i•ly (făm' ə lē) *or* (făm' lē) *noun, plural* **families** Parents and their children: *My family always goes on vacation together.*

fa•ther (fä' thər) *noun, plural* **fathers** The male parent of a child: *Gina's father took her to the doctor today.*

feat (fēt) *noun, plural* **feats** An act or deed that shows great bravery, skill, or strength: *Riding the bicycle ten miles was a feat.*

Feb•ru•ar•y (fĕb' rŏŏ ĕr' ē) *or* (fĕb' yŏŏ ĕr' ē) *noun* The second month of the year: *Groundhog Day comes in February.*

few (fyŏŏ) *adjective* **fewer, fewest** Not many: *There were only a few pieces left.*

fill (fĭl) *verb* **filled, filling** **1.** To make or become full: *I always fill the sugar bowl to the top.* **2.** To spread throughout: *My writing filled the pages of my diary.*

find (fīnd) *verb* **found** (found), **finding**
1. To look for and get: *I found my keys under my bed.* **2.** To meet with; come upon: *Polar bears are only found in the far north.*

fire (fīr) *noun, plural* **fires** Heat and light given off by burning something: *They saw the fire and ran for help.*

first (fûrst) *adjective* Coming before any other in time, place, or order: *This is my first pair of ice skates.* —*noun* Person or thing that is first: *Tyrel was first in line.*
Idiom. at first. In the beginning: *At first, Ellen was scared but then she got brave.*

floor (flôr) *or* (flōr) *noun, plural* **floors** The part of a room people walk on: *The floor squeaks when you walk on it.*

flour·ish (flûr′ ĭsh) *or* (flŭr′ ĭsh) *verb* **flourished, flourishing** To grow strongly and well: *The flowers flourish in the sunny garden.*

flow·er (flou′ ər) *noun, plural* **flowers** The part of the plant where seeds are made; the blossom: *This plant has yellow flowers.*

fly (flī) *verb* **flies, flew, flown, flying** To move through the air with wings: *I love to watch airplanes fly in and out of the airport.*

foot (fŏŏt) *noun, plural* **feet** The part of the leg on which a person or animal walks: *I put my shoe on the wrong foot.*

for·get (fər gĕt′) *or* (fôr gĕt′) *verb* **forgot** (fər gŏt′), **forgotten, forgetting** To be unable to remember: *Don't forget to study.*

for·got Look up **forget.**

fork (fôrk) *noun, plural* **forks** **1.** A tool used to pick up food: *I eat with a fork.* **2.** A place where something divides into more than one part: *When we came to the fork in the trail, we didn't know which way to go.*

found Look up **find.**

four (fôr) *noun* The number that follows three: *Two plus two is four.* —*adjective* Being one more than three in number: *There are four people in my family.*

Pronunciation Key

ă	pat	îr	deer	*th*	**th**is
ā	pay	ŏ	pot	ŭ	c**u**t
âr	care	ō	toe	ûr	**u**rge
ä	father	ô	paw, for	ə	**a**bout,
ĕ	pet	oi	noise		it**e**m,
ē	bee	ŏŏ	took		edibl**e**,
ĭ	pit	ōō	boot		gall**o**p,
ī	pie	ou	out		circ**u**s
		th	thin		

frag·ile (frăj′ əl) *or* (frăj′ īl) *adjective* Easy to break or damage: *The glass is fragile.*

frail (frāl) *adjective* **frailer, frailest**
1. Easily broken or damaged: *The very old chair is frail.* **2.** Not having strength; weak: *I was frail after my illness.*

free (frē) *adjective* **freer, freest 1.** Not under someone else's control: *The cat was free to roam around the neighborhood.* **2.** Without cost: *We won two free tickets.*

Fri·day (frī′ dē) *or* (frī′ dā′) *noun, plural* **Fridays** The sixth day of the week: *Our teacher didn't give us homework on Friday.*

friend (frĕnd) *noun, plural* **friends** A person one knows and likes: *My friend and I write letters to each other in a secret code.*

friend·li·ness (frĕnd′ lē nĭs) *noun* The manner or actions of a friend: *Aaron's friendliness makes everyone feel welcome.*

frog (frôg) *or* (frŏg) *noun, plural* **frogs** A small animal with webbed feet and smooth skin: *Frogs have strong legs.*

from (frŭm) *or* (frŏm) *or* (frəm) *preposition* **1.** Having as an origin: *I got a letter from my cousin.* **2.** Starting at: *The boys raced from school to their house.*

front (frŭnt) *noun, plural* **fronts** The part of something that faces forward: *There was a crowd in front of the music store.*

fron·tier (frŭn tîr′) or (frŭn′ tîr′) noun, plural **frontiers** **1.** The border between countries: *The family crossed the frontier between Mexico and the United States.* **2.** The far edge of a country where people are just beginning to live. *Pioneers lived on the wild frontier of the West.*

ful·fill (fŏol fĭl′) verb **fulfilled, fulfilling** To carry out, finish, or do what is called for: *He is fulfilling his promise.*

full (fŏol) adjective **fuller, fullest** Holding all that it can hold: *My stomach was full after dinner.*

fun·ny (fŭn′ ē) adjective **funnier, funniest** Causing laughter; amusing: *Ty's jokes are funny. Brad's jokes are funnier than mine. Angela's are the funniest.*

fur (fûr) noun, plural **furs** Thick, soft hair that covers certain animals: *My dog's fur keeps him warm in the winter.*

gar·den (gär′ dn) noun, plural **gardens** A piece of land used for growing vegetables and flowers: *We plant beans in the garden.*

gen·u·ine (jĕn′ yŏo ĭn) adjective **1.** Real: *A genuine ruby costs a lot of money.* **2.** Sincere; honest: *My aunt showed a genuine interest in my story.*

girl (gûrl) noun, plural **girls** A female child: *Hannah was the only girl on the team.*

glid·er (glī′ dər) noun, plural **gliders** An aircraft that flies without a motor and moves easily on currents of air: *The ride in the glider was fun.*

go (gō) verb **goes** (gōz), **went, gone, going** To move; travel: *Mary goes to the dentist every year.*

goes Look up **go.**

gold (gōld) noun A heavy, precious, yellow metal used for making jewelry and coins: *Will has a watch that is made of gold.*

good (gŏod) adjective **better, best** **1.** Having high quality: *To hike, you need a good pair of boots.* **2.** Desirable; pleasing: *We had good weather for our picnic. The weather last month was better than now. The weather in the spring was the best all year.*

gour·met (gŏor mā′) or (gŏor′ mā′) noun, plural **gourmets** A person who loves fine food and knows a great deal about it. —adjective Having to do with fine food: *Mother cooked a gourmet dinner.*

gov·ern (gŭv′ ərn) verb **governed, governing** To rule, control, direct, or manage: *He governed the country for a year.*

gray (grā) noun, plural **grays** Any color that is a mixture of black and white: *Do you like the color gray?* —adjective **grayer, grayest** Having the color gray: *I have a gray cat.*

great (grāt) adjective **greater, greatest** Wonderful; very good: *It would be great to travel from zoo to zoo. Of the two zoos, which is greater? This is the greatest zoo in the world.*

ground (ground) noun Soil; land: *The ground was covered with snow after the storm.*

guess (gĕs) verb **guessed, guessing** **1.** To form an opinion without enough knowledge: *We were guessing what the surprise would be.* **2.** To think; suppose: *I guess I'll just stay here.*

had·n't (hăd′ nt) The contraction of "had not": *I hadn't known him long before he moved away.*

hair (hâr) noun, plural **hairs** The thin, threadlike strands that grow from a person's or animal's skin: *Nan wears her long hair in a braid.*

half (hăf) *noun, plural* **halves** One of two equal parts: *Jenna ate half of her sandwich.*

ham·mer (hăm′ ər) *noun, plural* **hammers** A tool with an iron head used to drive in nails: *I need a hammer to put the birdhouse together.*

hand (hănd) *noun, plural* **hands** The part of the arm below the wrist: *I held the baby chick in my hands.* —*verb* **handed, handing** To pass with the hands: *I handed the teacher my story.*

hap·py (hăp′ ē) *adjective* **happier, happiest** Feeling pleased or joyful: *She was happy when she won the award.*

hard (härd) *adjective* **harder, hardest** Not easy: *This math test is too hard.* —*adverb* **harder, hardest** With energy or effort: *Dennis worked hard.*

has·n't (hăz′ ənt) The contraction of "has not": *Joey hasn't gone yet.*

have·n't (hăv′ ənt) The contraction of "have not": *I haven't heard from Delyn since she went to camp.*

head (hĕd) *noun, plural* **heads** The top part of the body that contains the brain, eyes, ears, nose, and mouth: *Jane put the hat on her head.* —*verb* **headed, heading** To go toward: *The bird headed south for the winter.*

hear (hîr) *verb* **heard, hearing** **1.** To be aware of sound: *Do you hear a noise in the attic?* **2.** To be told: *Emily and her class were about to hear the story of Daniel Boone.* • **Hear** sounds like **here.**

heart (härt) *noun, plural* **hearts** **1.** The organ in the chest that pumps blood through the body: *The doctor listened to my heart.* **2.** Courage and enthusiasm: *He put his heart into winning the game.*

hel·lo (hĕ lō′) *or* (hə lō′) *interjection* A greeting: *Sharon always answers the phone with a cheery, "Hello."*

help (hĕlp) *verb* **helped, helping** To aid or assist; to be useful: *Will you help me hang this picture? I helped Dee buy new jeans.*

Pronunciation Key

ă	pat	îr	deer	*th*	**th**is
ā	pay	ŏ	pot	ŭ	c**u**t
âr	care	ō	toe	ûr	**ur**ge
ä	father	ô	paw, for	ə	**a**bout,
ĕ	pet	oi	noise		item,
ē	bee	ŏŏ	took		edible,
ĭ	pit	ōō	boot		gall**o**p,
ī	pie	ou	**ou**t		circus
		th	**th**in		

here (hîr) *adverb* In this place or spot: *Cheri and I have been waiting here all afternoon.* —*noun* This place: *The ice cream truck is four blocks from here.* • **Here** sounds like **hear.**

he's (hēz) The contraction of "he is" or "he has": *He's the new music teacher.*

high (hī) *adjective* **higher, highest** Tall: *That pine tree is 25 feet high.* —*adverb* At or to a high point: *My balloon flew high up in the sky.*

hold (hōld) *verb* **held, holding 1.** To have and keep in the hand; grasp: *I have to hold my sister's hand when we go shopping.* **2.** To keep in a certain position: *Hold your head still.*

hole (hōl) *noun, plural* **holes** A hollow or empty place in something solid: *The pirates dug a hole and buried a treasure chest.* • **Hole** sounds like **whole.**

hop (hŏp) *verb* **hopped, hopping** To move by taking small jumps or skips: *The rabbit was hopping across the field.*

hope (hōp) *verb* **hoped, hoping** To wish for something: *I hope my grandmother feels better soon. Julia hoped she wouldn't be late for school.*

hot (hŏt) *adjective* **hotter, hottest** Very warm: *It is hotter outside today than it was yesterday. Tomorrow may be the hottest day of the year.*

hour (our) *noun, plural* **hours** A period of time equal to 60 minutes: *The bread will take one hour to bake.* • **Hour** sounds like **our.**

house (hous) *noun, plural* **houses** (hou′ zĭz) A building that people live in: *The Scouts met at my house.*

how'd (houd) The contraction of "how did": *How'd you tie the knot?*

hud·dle (hŭd′ l) *noun, plural* **huddles** A group or crowd that is closely gathered or packed together: *Our team plans the next play when we are in a huddle.* —*verb* **huddled, huddling** To gather close together: *The campers huddled in the tent.*

huge (hyōōj) *adjective* **huger, hugest** Very large; enormous: *The circus parade was led by a huge elephant.*

hun·dred (hŭn′ drĭd) *noun, plural* **hundreds** The number that follows 99, written 100 in numerals: *Did you know that 100 is equal to 50 plus 50?* —*adjective* Being one more than 99 in number: *There are 100 pages in this book.*

I'd (īd) The contraction of "I had," "I would," or "I should": *I'd better get home before dark. I'd rather eat brownies than bake them.*

I'll (īl) The contraction of "I will" or "I shall": *I'll never remember everyone's name.*

I'm (īm) The contraction of "I am": *I'm sure I will make the team.*

in·come (ĭn′ kŭm′) *noun, plural* **incomes** Money that a person receives for work or from other things during a certain period of time: *Roderick wants to earn an income as a teacher.*

in·dex (ĭn′ dĕks′) *noun, plural* **indexes** An alphabetical list of names and subjects at the end of a book that gives the page or pages where each can be found: *Mary looked in the index to find the pages where butterflies are described.*

in·side (ĭn sīd′) *or* (ĭn′ sīd′) *noun, plural* **insides** The inner part: *We painted the inside of the house.* —*preposition* (ĭn sīd′) Into: *She put her hand inside the grab bag.*

in·spire (ĭn spīr′) *verb* **inspired, inspiring 1.** To move the mind, feelings, or imagination: *Nature may inspire the artist.* **2.** To move to action: *He inspired me to try.*

in·stall (ĭn stôl′) *verb* **installed, installing** To put in place for use or service: *My father will install a new furnace.*

in·struct (ĭn strŭkt′) *verb* **instructed, instructing** To teach or show how to do something: *Will Bruce instruct the tennis class?*

is·n't (ĭz′ ənt) The contraction of "is not": *This isn't my lunch box.*

it's (ĭts) The contraction of "it is" or "it has": *It's time for lunch.*

I've (īv) The contraction of "I have": *I've never seen a movie that scared me so much.*

jab (jăb) *verb* **jabbed, jabbing** To poke with something pointed: *Why are you jabbing me with your finger?*

Jan·u·ar·y (jăn′ yōō ĕr′ ē) *noun* The first month of the year: *January has 31 days.*

jog (jŏg) *verb* **jogged, jogging** To run slowly: *My mom jogged one mile.*

join (join) *verb* **joined, joining 1.** To put together: *We joined hands and made a circle.* **2.** To take part with others: *Will you join us for a swim across the lake?*

joke (jōk) *noun, plural* **jokes** Something funny said or done to make someone laugh: *Roberto makes everyone laugh with his elephant jokes.* —*verb* **joked, joking** To do or say something as a joke: *I was only joking.*

joy (joi) *noun, plural* **joys** A feeling of great happiness: *My dog jumps for joy when he sees me.*

June (jōon) *noun* The sixth month of the year: *School is over in June.*

just (jŭst) *adjective* Fair: *Tim didn't think the teacher was just in giving a surprise test.* —*adverb* At that moment: *Just when he fell asleep, the phone rang.*

keep (kēp) *verb* **kept, keeping 1.** To have; own: *You may keep the picture.* **2.** To continue in a certain condition or place; to stay: *I kept the hamster in a cage.*

kept Look up **keep.**

key (kē) *noun, plural* **keys 1.** A piece of shaped metal used to open a lock: *I lost my key, so I couldn't get in the house.* **2.** The most important part: *Exercise is the key to good health.*

kick (kĭk) *verb* **kicked, kicking** To hit with the foot: *I saw the horse kick the door.*

kind¹ (kīnd) *adjective* **kinder, kindest** Thoughtful; helpful: *The nurse is very kind.*

kind² (kīnd) *noun, plural* **kinds** A type; variety: *What kind of music do you like?*

knew Look up **know.**

know (nō) *verb* **knew** (nōo) *or* (nyōo), **known, knowing 1.** To be certain of the facts: *I know you are hiding under the stairs.* **2.** To be familiar with: *Penny knew everyone.*

la•bor (lā′ bər) *noun, plural* **labors** Hard work: *Making a new garden took much labor.* —*verb* **labored, laboring** To work hard: *Jacob labored for hours to do the math problems.*

late (lāt) *adjective* **later, latest** After the usual or expected time: *The bus was late.*

Pronunciation Key

ă	pat	îr	deer	*th*	this
ā	pay	ŏ	pot	ŭ	cut
âr	care	ō	toe	ûr	urge
ä	father	ô	paw, for	ə	about,
ĕ	pet	oi	noise		item,
ē	bee	ŏŏ	took		edible,
ĭ	pit	ōō	boot		gallop,
ī	pie	ou	out		circus
		th	thin		

laugh (lăf) *verb* **laughed, laughing** To make sounds and move your face to show joy or amusement: *I laugh at his jokes.*

learn (lûrn) *verb* **learned** or **learnt, learning** To gain knowledge or skill: *Erma wants to learn how to speak Spanish.*

light¹ (līt) *noun, plural* **lights** Anything that gives off the energy by which we see, such as a lamp: *Please turn off the light.*

light² (līt) *adjective* **lighter, lightest** Not heavy: *The box was light because it was empty.*

like¹ (līk) *verb* **liked, liking 1.** To be fond of someone or something: *I have always liked my cousin, Sal.* **2.** To enjoy: *Ida liked to dance.*

like² (līk) *preposition.* **1.** Similar to: *Harriet's coat is just like mine.* **2.** In the mood for: *I feel like going for a walk.*

line (līn) *noun, plural* **lines** A long row of people or things: *The line was too long.*

li•on (lī′ ən) *noun, plural* **lions** A large wild cat from Africa or Asia: *We heard the lion roar.*

lit•tle (lĭt′ l) *adjective* **littler, littlest,** or **least** Small in size or quantity: *My kitten is very little.*

loaf¹ (lōf) *noun, plural* **loaves** Bread baked in one piece or shape: *I sliced the loaf of bread that I'd just made.*

loaf² (lōf) *verb* **loafed, loafing** To be lazy: *My dog loafs around the house.*

long (lông) *or* (lŏng) *adjective* **longer, longest** Not short; great in length or time: *The school play was very long. Your fingers are longer than mine. That is the longest snake I have ever seen.* —*adverb* **longer, longest** For a great amount of time: *We worked on our math problems all day long.*

loss (lôs) *or* (lŏs) *noun, plural* **losses** The act or fact of not winning something: *Our hockey team has ten losses.*

love•ly (lŭv′ lē) *adjective* **lovelier, loveliest** Beautiful: *The flowers look lovely.*

lug•gage (lŭg′ ĭj) *noun* Suitcases and bags that a person takes on a trip: *The luggage is very heavy.*

lunch (lŭnch) *noun, plural* **lunches** The midday meal: *Ethan always has a sandwich for lunch.*

main•tain (mān tān′) *verb* **maintained, maintaining 1.** To keep in good condition: *Mark will help maintain the garden.* **2.** To continue to have; keep.

mall (môl) *or* (mäl) *noun, plural* **malls** A shopping center: *Mom took me to the mall.*

man•y (měn′ ē) *adjective* **more, most** A large number of: *Many animals live in this forest.*

March (märch) *noun* The third month of the year: *March is the best month for flying kites.*

mar•ket (mär′ kĭt) *noun, plural* **markets** A place where goods are bought and sold: *We always go to the market for fresh vegetables.*

match¹ (măch) *verb* **matched, matching** To be alike; to look alike: *Socks need to match.*

match² (măch) *noun, plural* **matches** A small stick of wood or cardboard that bursts into flame when rubbed: *Dad lit the campfire with matches.*

mat•ter (măt′ ər) *noun, plural* **matters** Problem or trouble: *What's the matter with your goldfish?* —*verb* **mattered, mattering** To be of importance: *Does it matter to you if we go to the store first?*

May (mā) *noun* The fifth month of the year: *Those flowers always bloom in May.*

meat (mēt) *noun* The flesh of animals used as food: *We had meat and salad for dinner.* • **Meat** sounds like **meet**.

meet (mēt) *verb* **met, meeting** To come together; come face to face: *Meet me on the corner after school.* • **Meet** sounds like **meat**.

meet•ing (mē′ tĭng) *noun, plural* **meetings** A coming together for some common purpose: *The lion called a meeting of all the animals in his kingdom.*

me•te•or (mē′ tē ər) *or* (mē′ tē ôr′) *noun, plural* **meteors** Matter from space that forms a bright trail or streak of light as it burns when it enters the earth's atmosphere: *We saw two meteors last night.*

mile (mīl) *noun, plural* **miles** A unit of distance equal to 5,280 feet or 1,609.34 meters: *The baseball field is two miles away.*

mind (mīnd) *noun, plural* **minds** The part of a person that thinks, feels, learns, etc.: *Mr. Sosa, my science teacher, says I have a good mind.* —*verb* **minded, minding** To object to: *Would you mind if I borrowed your pencil?*

mine (mīn) *pronoun* The thing or things belonging to me: *That's Bobby's bed, and this one is mine.*

mis•er•y (mĭz′ ə rē) *noun, plural* **miseries** Great pain or unhappiness: *The tornado caused misery for everyone in its path.*

moist•en (moi′ sən) *verb* **moistened, moistening** To make slightly wet or damp: *The rain moistened the garden.*

Mon•day (mŭn′ dē) *or* (mŭn′ dā′) *noun, plural* **Mondays** The second day of the week: *Sometimes it's hard to wake up on Monday.*

mon•ey (mŭn′ ē) *noun* Coins and bills printed by a government and used to pay for things: *Judy is saving her money to buy a radio.*

month (mŭnth) *noun* One of the 12 parts that a year is divided into: *My birthday is this month.*

morn•ing (môr′ nĭng) *noun, plural* **mornings** The early part of the day: *I have cereal for breakfast every morning.*

most (mōst) *adjective* The greatest amount: *The team that gets the most runs will win.* —*noun* The larger part: *I like most of the people in this club.* Look up **many, much.**

moth•er (mŭth′ ər) *noun, plural* **mothers** A female parent of a child: *Percy's mother writes articles for magazines.*

move (mōōv) *verb* **moved, moving** To change from one position to another: *Mom is always moving the furniture around.* —*noun, plural* **moves** The act of moving: *The frog made his move and caught the fly.*

much (mŭch) **more, most** *adjective* Great in amount: *I have much work to do.* —*adverb* Greatly; to a large degree: *Frank is much taller than his brother.*

must (mŭst) *helping verb* Will have to; should: *You must wear a smock in art class.*

must•n't (mŭs′ ənt) The contraction of "must not": *Carla mustn't have heard the dinner bell.*

near (nîr) *preposition* **nearer, nearest** Not far from; close to: *Ruben lives near his grandparents.*

neck•tie (nĕk′ tī′) *noun, plural* **neckties** A band of cloth worn around the neck and tied in a knot in front: *Nick wears neckties with all his shirts.*

Pronunciation Key

ă	pat	îr	deer	*th*	this
ā	pay	ŏ	pot	ŭ	cut
âr	care	ō	toe	ûr	urge
ä	father	ô	paw, for	ə	about,
ĕ	pet	oi	noise		item,
ē	bee	ŏŏ	took		edible,
ĭ	pit	ōō	boot		gallop,
ī	pie	ou	out		circus
		th	thin		

need (nēd) *verb* **needed, needing** To require; must have: *I need a collar for my dog.*

nev•er (nĕv′ ər) *adverb* Not at any time: *Ben never gives up.*

news (nōōz) *or* (nyōōz) *noun* (used with a singular verb) Recent events or information: *The news about the earthquake is shocking.*

next (nĕkst) *adjective* **1.** Coming right after: *We'll get on the next train.* **2.** Nearest in position: *Mom is in the next room.*

nice (nīs) *adjective* **nicer, nicest** Pleasant; agreeable: *It was a nice evening for a walk.*

night (nīt) *noun, plural* **nights** The time between sunset and sunrise: *On a clear night, it's fun to look at the stars.*

noise (noiz) *noun, plural* **noises** A sound, especially if loud: *We heard a loud noise.*

none (nŭn) *pronoun* Not any; not one: *None of my friends can ski.*

noon (nōōn) *noun* Midday; 12 o'clock in the middle of the day: *We'll eat at noon.*

north (nôrth) *noun* The direction toward the North Pole: *A compass needle always points to the north.* —*adverb* Toward the north: *Clifton walked north to go into town.*

noth•ing (nŭth′ ĭng) *pronoun* **1.** Not anything: *Nothing the clown did made the child smile.* **2.** Of no importance: *It's nothing at all.*

No•vem•ber (nō vĕm′ bər) *noun* The eleventh month of the year: *We eat turkey in November.*

num·ber (**nŭm′** bər) *noun, plural* **numbers** **1.** A figure or numeral that identifies something: *His football number is 12.* **2.** Amount: *Tell me the number of marbles you have.*

o'clock (ə **klŏk′**) *adverb* According to the clock: *My favorite TV show begins at 7 o'clock.*

Oc·to·ber (ŏk **tō′** bər) *noun* The tenth month of the year: *Halloween is the last day of October.*

off (ôf) *or* (ŏf) *adverb* Not on; removed: *He took his hat off.* —*preposition* Away from a place: *She dived off the pier.*

oil (oil) *noun* **1.** A greasy liquid or fat that easily becomes liquid: *We dropped the popcorn into the hot oil.* **2.** Petroleum: *They drill for oil.*

one (wŭn) *noun, plural* **ones** A number, written 1: *One plus two equals three.* —*pronoun* A particular person or thing: *One of my turtles is missing.* • **One** sounds like **won.**

on·ly (**ōn′** lē) *adjective* Sole; without others: *This is my only brother, Ricardo.* —*adverb* Just; merely: *Philip was 14, but he acted as if he were only 4.*

o·pen (**ō′** pən) *verb* **opened, opening** To cause something to be no longer closed: *I couldn't wait to open the box that was for me.*

or·na·ment (**ôr′** nə mənt) *noun, plural* **ornaments** An object that makes something more beautiful: *The tree ornament is blue and red.*

oth·er (**ŭ**th**′** ər) *adjective* Different: *I have other things to do.* —*pronoun, plural* **others** The remaining people or things: *Mom carried the big box and I carried all the others.*

our (our) *adjective* Of or belonging to us: *Our dog followed us to school.* • **Our** sounds like **hour.**

o·ver (**ō′** vər) *preposition* **1.** Above; higher than: *It was raining, but at least we had a tent over our heads.* **2.** On the surface of; upon: *Teddy spilled raisins all over the floor.* —*adjective* Finished: *The play is over.*

owl (oul) *noun, plural* **owls** A kind of bird with a flat face, large eyes, and a short, hooked beak. Owls make a hooting sound: *The hoot of the owl scares some people.*

page¹ (pāj) *noun, plural* **pages** One side of a sheet paper in a book: *For homework I had to read pages 17 and 18 in my science book.*

page² (pāj) *noun, plural* **pages** A person who runs errands or delivers messages: *The page brought a message to my hotel room.* —*verb* **paged, paging** To call for someone in a public place: *When Tom got lost in the airport, his mother paged him on the loudspeaker.*

paint (pānt) *noun, plural* **paints** Coloring matter mixed with oil or water: *John made a picture with 12 different colors of paint.* —*verb* **painted, painting** **1.** To cover or coat something with paint: *Alice painted her skateboard blue.* **2.** To make a picture using paint: *He liked to paint pictures of his dog, Igor.*

pa·per (**pā′** pər) *noun, plural* **papers** **1.** A material made from wood pulp or rags. Paper is usually in the form of thin sheets. It is used for writing, drawing, printing, wrapping packages, and covering walls: *Tony used up all the paper in the house writing letters to his pen pal.* **2.** A newspaper: *I read about the parade in the paper.*

pa·trol (pə **trōl′**) *noun, plural* **patrols** A person or group of people who move about an area to make sure everything is all right: *The highway patrol makes sure people drive safely.*

pay (pā) *verb* **paid, paying 1.** To give money for something bought or for work done: *I had to pay 80 dollars for my new bicycle.* **2.** To give, make, or do: *I always pay attention in dance class.* —*noun* Money given for work done: *My pay was ten dollars.*

pen·ny (pĕn′ ē) *noun, plural* **pennies** One cent: *This dollar equals 100 pennies.*

peo·ple (pē′ pəl) *noun, plural* **people** Human beings: *Many people came to the party.*

place (plās) *noun, plural* **places** A particular spot: *People travel from many places to see the rodeo.* —*verb* **placed, placing** To put in a particular location or area: *I placed the toys on the shelf.* **Idiom. take place.** To happen: *When will the wedding take place?*

plaid (plăd) *noun, plural* **plaids** A design of stripes of different widths and colors that cross each other to make squares: *The plaid of his shirt was red, blue, and gold.*

please (plēz) *verb* **pleased, pleasing 1.** To give pleasure or happiness to; to be agreeable to: *He was pleased when I took him to the circus.* **2.** Be so kind as to: *Please close the door.*

point (point) *noun, plural* **points** Sharp or narrowed end of something; the tip: *I broke the point on my pencil.* —*verb* **pointed, pointing** To call attention to with the finger; to show.

poi·son·ous (poi′ zə nəs) *adjective* Having poison in it or having the effects of poison: *We were careful not to step on a poisonous snake.*

poor (po͝or) *adjective* **poorer, poorest 1.** Having little or no money: *She was too poor to go to the movies with her friends.* **2.** Needing pity: *The poor kitten was lost.*

pop·corn (pŏp′ kôrn′) *noun* A kind of corn that pops open and puffs up when heated: *I like watching popcorn pop.*

Pronunciation Key

ă	pat	îr	deer	*th*	this
ā	pay	ŏ	pot	ŭ	cut
âr	care	ō	toe	ûr	urge
ä	father	ô	paw, for	ə	about,
ĕ	pet	oi	noise		item,
ē	bee	o͝o	took		edible,
ĭ	pit	o͞o	boot		gallop,
ī	pie	ou	out		circus
		th	thin		

pour (pôr) *verb* **poured, pouring 1.** To cause to flow in a stream: *I always pour maple syrup over my pancakes.* **2.** A heavy rain: *We opened our umbrellas as it started to pour.*

pow·er (pou′ ər) *noun, plural* **powers** Strength or force: *This runner has plenty of power in her legs.*

pret·ty (prĭt′ ē) *adjective* **prettier, prettiest** Pleasing; attractive; appealing: *The sunset was very pretty.*

prob·lem (prŏb′ ləm) *noun, plural* **problems** Something or someone that is hard to understand or deal with: *Matt's problem was that he was tired.*

pull (po͝ol) *verb* **pulled, pulling** To draw something toward oneself: *Pull on the rope.*

pur·sue (pər so͞o′) *verb* **pursued, pursuing 1.** To chase or follow in order to catch: *The cat pursued the mouse.* **2.** To keep trying to reach: *I will pursue my goals.*

put (po͝ot) *verb* **put, putting** To place; to set: *Allen put the cookies in the cookie jar.*

Q

quart (kwôrt) *noun, plural* **quarts** A unit of measure equal to one quarter of a gallon: *I drank a quart of juice.*

queen (kwēn) *noun, plural* **queens 1.** A woman who rules over a country: *Queen Elizabeth rules Great Britain.* **2.** The wife of a king: *The queen lived in a castle.*

231

rain (rān) *noun* Drops of water that fall from the clouds: *The rain washed away the footprints in the dirt.* —*verb* **rained, raining** To fall in drops of water from the clouds: *It had rained all night.*

read (rēd) *verb* **read** (rĕd), **reading** To look at and get the meaning of something written or printed: *Every day I read the comics. I've already read the comics today.*

read·y (rĕd′ē) *adjective* **readier, readiest** Prepared to do something: *Tara was packed and ready to go.*

re·joice (rĭ jois′) *verb* **rejoiced, rejoicing** To show or feel great joy: *We rejoice when our team wins.*

right (rīt) *adjective* **1.** Opposite the left side: *I throw a ball with my right arm.* **2.** Correct; true; just: *Being truthful is the right thing to do.* —*adverb* Straight on; directly: *I walked right into a wall.* • **Right** sounds like **write.**

riv·er (rĭv′ər) *noun, plural* **rivers** A large stream of water that flows into a lake, ocean, sea, or another river: *My dad and I go fishing in the river.*

road (rōd) *noun, plural* **roads** An open way for travel between two or more places: *Do you remember how Dorothy followed the yellow brick road to Oz?*

ro·dent (rōd′ nt) *noun, plural* **rodents** Any of a large group of animals that have large front teeth used for gnawing, such as mice, rats, squirrels, and beavers: *We try to keep rodents out of the house.*

ro·de·o (rō′ dē ō′) *or* (ro dā′ ō) *noun, plural* **rodeos** A show where people use their skill in contests such as riding horses and roping cattle: *It is fun to go to a rodeo.*

roy·al (roi′ əl) *adjective* **1.** Of or having to do with kings or queens: *The prince was a member of the royal family.* **2.** Fit for a king or queen; splendid: *The queen lived in a royal palace.*

safe (sāf) *adjective* **safer, safest** Free from danger or harm: *Keep your money in a safe place.*

said Look up **say.**

sail (sāl) *noun, plural* **sails** A piece of strong material spread to catch the wind and make a boat move: *As the wind filled the sails, the sailboat moved faster.* —*verb* **sailed, sailing 1.** To travel across the water on a ship: *The ship is going to sail across the ocean to Europe.* **2.** To steer a boat: *I sailed the boat across the lake all by myself.*

Sat·ur·day (săt′ ər dē) *or* (săt′ ər dā′) *noun, plural* **Saturdays** The seventh day of the week: *Mom took us to the baseball game on Saturday.*

sau·sage (sô′ sĭj) *noun, plural* **sausages** Chopped meat that is mixed with spices and stuffed into a thin tube-shaped casing: *We had sausage for breakfast.*

save (sāv) *verb* **saved, saving 1.** To free from danger or harm: *Marie saved Ellen from falling off the swing.* **2.** To avoid wasting: *I took the bus instead of walking to save time.*

say (sā) *verb* **says** (sĕz), **said** (sĕd), **saying** To speak; to talk: *Grandma says it's time for dinner.*

scheme (skēm) *noun, plural* **schemes** A plan or plot for doing something: *Ling has a scheme for doing her homework.*

school¹ (skool) *noun, plural* **schools** A place of teaching and learning: *We learned about Japan in school.*

school² (skool) *noun, plural* **schools** A large group of fish that swim together: *While we were fishing, a school of minnows swam by.*

sea (sē) *noun, plural* **seas** The great body of water that covers about three-fourths of the earth's surface; ocean: *Whales live in the sea.*

seam (sēm) *noun, plural* **seams** A line or fold formed by sewing together two pieces of cloth or other material: *The seam on the shirt ripped.*

sec•ond[1] (sĕk′ ənd) *noun, plural* **seconds** A unit of time equal to ¹/₆₀ of one minute: *Janet finished the test in 3 minutes and 10 seconds flat.*

sec•ond[2] (sĕk′ ənd) *adjective* Next after the first: *Mike came in first in the race, and I came in second.*

send (sĕnd) *verb* **sent** (sĕnt), **sending** To cause or order to go: *Dad sent me to the store to buy ice cream for dessert.*

sent Look up **send.** • **Sent** sounds like **cent.**

Sep•tem•ber (sĕp tĕm′ bər) *noun* The ninth month of the year. September has 30 days: *In September we go back to school.*

shake (shāk) *verb* **shook** (shŏŏk), **shaken, shaking 1.** To tremble or quiver: *I was so scared that my whole body began to shake.* **2.** To cause to move: *The boys shook the tree, and all the leaves fell off.*

shak•y (shā′ kē) *adjective* **shakier, shakiest 1.** Trembling; quivering: *Her voice was shakier than mine.* **2.** Not firm; likely to break down: *Kevin's bike is the shakiest I have ever ridden.*

sharp (shärp) *adjective* **sharper, sharpest 1.** Something having a thin, cutting edge or point: *Anna needed a sharp pencil to do her homework. My pencil is sharper than Ben's. Taylor's pencil is the sharpest of all.* **2.** Quickly aware of things; keen: *Owls' sharp eyesight helps them to see in the dark.*

she'll (shēl) The contraction of "she will": *My mother says she'll pick us up after practice.*

Pronunciation Key

ă	pat	îr	deer	*th*	**this**
ā	pay	ŏ	pot	ŭ	cut
âr	care	ō	toe	ûr	urge
ä	father	ô	paw, for	ə	about,
ĕ	pet	oi	noise		item,
ē	bee	ŏŏ	took		edible,
ĭ	pit	ōō	boot		gallop,
ī	pie	ou	out		circus
		th	thin		

she's (shēz) The contraction of "she is" or "she has": *She's going to the bookstore.*

shine (shīn) *verb* **shone** (shōn) **shined, shining 1.** To give off or reflect light: *Why are you shining the flashlight in my eyes?* **2.** To polish: *I shined my shoes today.*

shook (shŏŏk) Look up **shake.**

shop (shŏp) *noun, plural* **shops** A store; a place where goods are sold: *Don's favorite shop is Toy Joy.* —*verb* **shopped, shopping** To visit stores to buy things: *My brother and I are shopping for a pet frog.*

should (shŏŏd) *helping verb* Ought to; have a duty to: *I should practice the piano every day.*

should•n't (shŏŏd′ nt) The contraction of "should not": *You shouldn't tease your little sister.*

shove (shŭv) *verb* **shoved, shoving** To push roughly: *When Mom came into my room, I shoved the present under the bed.* —*noun, plural* **shoves** A push: *My dog wouldn't move, so I gave him a little shove.*

show (shō) *verb* **showed, shown, showing 1.** To make known; to reveal: *Please show me the way home.* **2.** To present for others to see: *Let's show everyone our bowling trophy.* —*noun, plural* **shows** Any kind of public performance, entertainment, or display: *Ms. Cook's class put on an art show at school.*

shrewd (shrōōd) *adjective* **shrewder, shrewdest** Clever and smart: *The shrewd buyer looked for the best price.*

233

size (sīz) *noun, plural* **sizes** The height, width, or length of a thing: *Billy and Vernon have always been the same size.*

sketch (skĕch) *noun, plural* **sketches** A rough, quick drawing: *The sketch showed a bare tree.* —*verb* **sketched, sketching** To make a sketch: *She sketched quickly.*

sky (skī) *noun, plural* **skies** The air high above the earth; the heavens: *I fly my kite high up in the sky.*

sky•line (skī′ līn′) *noun, plural* **skylines** **1.** The outline of buildings or other objects as seen against the sky: *We could see the city's skyline from the airplane.* **2.** The line at which the earth and sky seem to meet.

sleep (slēp) *noun* A natural rest of body and mind; state of not being awake: *I'm so tired that I could use a week of sleep.* —*verb* **slept** (slĕpt), **sleeping** To be in or to fall into a state of sleep: *My dad is sleeping in his chair.*

sleep•y (slē′ pē) *adjective* **sleepier, sleepiest** Ready for sleep; drowsy: *When I am sleepy, I start to yawn.*

slept Look up **sleep.**

slow (slō) *adverb* **slower, slowest** Not quick: *Bobby walks slower than a turtle.* —*verb* **slowed, slowing** To cause to move slow or slower: *Please slow down.*

slump (slŭmp) *verb* **slumped, slumping** To fall or sink down suddenly: *Mother told me not to slump in my chair at dinner.*

smile (smīl) *verb* **smiled, smiling** To show an expression of happiness by turning the corners of the mouth upward; grinning: *The boy was smiling at his new puppy.*

smudge (smŭj) *noun, plural* **smudges** A dirty mark or smear: *The birthday card had a black smudge on it.* —*verb* **smudged, smudging** To make dirty or smeared.

sneeze (snēz) *verb* **sneezed, sneezing** To force air to pass suddenly with force from the nose and mouth. A tickling inside the nose causes a person to sneeze: *When John caught a cold, he sneezed for two days.*

snow (snō) *noun, plural* **snows** Soft white flakes of frozen water vapor that form in the sky and fall to the earth: *Jeremy loved to ride his sled in the snow.* —*verb* **snowed, snowing** To fall as snow.

sock (sŏk) *noun, plural* **socks** A short stocking reaching no higher than the knee: *I stepped in a puddle and got my socks wet.*

sog•gy (sô′ gē) *or* (sŏ′ gē) *adjective* **soggier, soggiest** Very wet; soaked: *My shoes were soggy after I played in the rain.*

soil[1] (soil) *noun* The loose top layer of the earth's surface in which plants grow: *My class planted a little tree in the soil.*

soil[2] (soil) *verb* **soiled, soiling** To make dirty: *Jane soiled her clean shirt.*

so•lo (sō′ lō) *adjective* Done by one person alone: *The pilot made her first solo flight.* —*noun, plural* **solos** Music that one person plays or sings all alone.

some (sŭm) *adjective* A certain number of: *Some people like pizza, and some people don't.* • **Some** sounds like **sum.**

some•bod•y (sŭm′ bŏd′ ē) *pronoun* A person not known or named: *Somebody lost a hat.*

some•thing (sŭm′ thĭng) *pronoun* A particular thing that is not named or known: *I want something good to eat.*

sor•ry (sŏr′ ē) *adjective* **sorrier, sorriest** Feeling sadness, regret, or pity: *Ms. Kyoto was sorry that she lost her sister's book.*

sound (sound) *noun, plural* **sounds** Something that is heard; sensation made by vibrations in the air and picked up by the ear: *We were surprised to hear a thumping sound.*

spend (spĕnd) *verb* **spent** (spĕnt), **spending** **1.** To pay out money: *He spent a lot of money for a new bat.* **2.** To pass time: *Katy spent the whole day at the carnival.*

spent Look up **spend**.

spin•ach (spĭn′ ĭch) *noun* A vegetable with dark green leaves. *I ate spinach for lunch.*

spoil (spoil) *verb* **spoiled** *or* **spoilt, spoiling** **1.** To ruin or damage: *The rain spoiled the class picnic.* **2.** To become unfit for use: *Milk will spoil if it isn't kept cold.*

sport (spôrt) *noun, plural* **sports** A game or contest requiring physical activity: *My favorite sport is soccer.*

spring (sprĭng) *noun, plural* **springs** **1.** The season before summer: *In the spring, flowers bloom.* **2.** A place where water flows to the surface: *Fish swim in the spring.*

stair (stâr) *noun, plural* **stairs** A step in a flight of steps: *Tom ran down the stairs.*

stand (stand) *verb* **stood, standing** To rise to be on one's feet: *He stood up and yawned.*

star (stär) *noun, plural* **stars** **1.** Any heavenly body, other than the moon or planets, seen from Earth. *A star shown brightly.* **2.** A famous person in any field or profession: *She is a movie star.*

starch (stärch) *noun, plural* **starches** **1.** White food matter that is made and stored in plants: *Corn has starch in it.* **2.** A product that is used to make cloth stiff.

start (stärt) *verb* **started, starting** To begin to go somewhere or do something: *Let's start a soccer club.*

stood Look up **stand**.

stop (stŏp) *verb* **stopped, stopping** To cease; to come to a halt: *When the rain stopped, Steven went out to play.*

storm (stôrm) *noun, plural* **storms** Strong winds accompanied by rain, hail, sand, or snow: *We saw a lot of lightning during the storm.*

Pronunciation Key

ă	pat	îr	deer	*th*	**th**is
ā	pay	ŏ	pot	ŭ	cut
âr	care	ō	toe	ûr	urge
ä	father	ô	paw, for	ə	about,
ĕ	pet	oi	noise		item,
ē	bee	ŏŏ	took		edible,
ĭ	pit	ōō	boot		gallop,
ī	pie	ou	out		circus
		th	thin		

sto•ry (stôr′ ē) *noun, plural* **stories** **1.** An account of something that has happened: *I read a true story.* **2.** A tale of fiction: *Phil told his sister a story.*

street (strēt) *noun, plural* **streets** A road in a city or town that is usually lined with buildings: *My house is on this street.*

strong (strông) *adjective* **stronger, strongest** Having much power or strength: *Sled dogs are strong animals. Horses are stronger. Elephants are the strongest.*

stun (stŭn) *verb* **stunned, stunning** **1.** To daze or make unconscious: *Jack was stunned when he bumped his head.* **2.** To shock: *Josh was stunned by the news.*

sub•tract (səb trăkt′) *verb* **subtracted, subtracting** To take away: *I subtracted two cents from eight cents, and the total was six cents.*

such (sŭch) *adjective* Of this kind or that kind: *I knew you'd wear such shoes.* —*adverb* Especially: *That was such a nice party.*

sum (sŭm) *noun, plural* **sums** The number you get when you add two or more numbers: *The sum of 5 and 6 is 11.*
• **Sum** sounds like **some.**

sum•mer (sŭm′ ər) *noun, plural* **summers** The warmest season of the year. Summer comes between spring and fall.

sun (sŭn) *noun* The star around which Earth and other planets revolve. The sun is the source of Earth's light and heat: *I wake up when the sun rises in the morning.*
• **Sun** sounds like **son.**

Sun·day (sŭn′ dē) *or* (sŭn′ dā′) *noun, plural* **Sundays** The first day of the week: *On Sunday Inga went to church.*

sun·ny (sŭn′ ē) *adjective* **sunnier, sunniest** Having much sun: *It was a sunny day at the beach.*

sup·per (sŭp′ ər) *noun, plural* **suppers** The evening meal or the last meal of the day: *My family ate supper at a very special restaurant.*

sure (sho͝or) *adjective* **surer, surest** Feeling certain; having no doubt: *Are you sure you don't want a piece of cake?*

sur·geon (sûr′ jən) *noun, plural* **surgeons** A doctor who treats injuries and diseases by cutting into the body and removing or repairing parts of it: *The surgeon operated on my foot.*

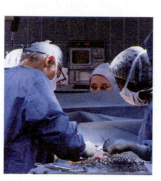

T

ta·ble (tā′ bəl) *noun, plural* **tables** A piece of furniture having a flat top supported by legs: *Lunch is on the table.*

take (tāk) *verb* **took** (to͝ok), **taken, taking 1.** To get; accept: *Did you take the book on the table?* **2.** To carry to a different place: *I am taking your suitcase upstairs.*

talk (tôk) *verb* **talked, talking** To speak; say words: *We were talking about Mark when he walked in.* —*noun, plural* **talks 1.** An informal speech: *I gave a talk in my class.* **2.** A rumor: *There's talk that Tia is ill.*

tall (tôl) *adjective* **taller, tallest 1.** Of more than average height: *My dad says I am tall. My brother is taller than I am. Mom is the tallest one in our family.* **2.** Hard to believe; exaggerated: *Who would believe that tall story?*

team (tēm) *noun, plural* **teams 1.** Two or more animals harnessed together to work: *The team of horses pulled the plow.* **2.** A group of people playing on the same side in a game: *The whole school came to watch our team win.*

teen·ag·er (tēn′ ā′ jər) *noun, plural* **teenagers** A person who is between the ages of thirteen and nineteen: *My older sister is a teenager.*

test (tĕst) *noun, plural* **tests 1.** A series of questions that judge a person's skill or knowledge: *I studied hard to pass my spelling test.* **2.** A way to find out the quality of something: *Lifting weights is a test of your strength.* —*verb* **tested, testing** To put to a test; to try out: *I tested the yo-yo.*

thank (thăngk) *verb* **thanked, thanking** To say that one is grateful or pleased: *The boys and girls thanked the magician for the show.*

them (thĕm) *or* (thəm) *pronoun* Persons, things, or animals spoken or written about: *We ate the cookies after we baked them.*

then (thĕn) *adverb* **1.** At the time: *I used to sleep with a teddy bear, but I was only a baby then.* **2.** After that: *We saw lightning flash, and then we heard the thunder roar.* **3.** A time mentioned: *Go finish your homework, and by then dinner will be ready.*

there'd (thârd) The contraction for "there would" or "there had": *There'd be ten people at the party if they all came.*

there'll (thârl) The contraction for "there will": *There'll be a baseball game tomorrow.*

these Look up **this.**

they (thā) *pronoun* **1.** The people, animals, or things named before: *Mr. Martin gave us six arithmetic problems, and they were all hard.* **2.** People in general: *They used to think the world was flat.*

they'd (thād) The contraction of "they had" or "they would": *They'd already eaten.*

they'll (*th*āl) The contraction of "they will" or "they shall": *Gino and Bonnie said they'll bring the cake to the party.*

they've (*th*āv) The contraction of "they have": *The boys say they've never gone fishing.*

thing (thĭng) *noun, plural* **things** **1.** Any object or substance that cannot be named exactly: *What is that green thing on the floor?* **2.** An act; a deed: *Hitting that home run was the best thing I ever did.*

think (thĭngk) *verb* **thought, thinking** **1.** To use the mind to come to an opinion: *I think I should go home now.* **2.** To have in mind: *Julia thinks she would like to be a doctor.*

third (thûrd) *noun, plural* **thirds** One of three equal parts: *Roger ate a third of the pizza.* —*adjective* Next after second.

this (*th*ĭs) *adjective, plural* **these** (*th*ēz) Being a thing or person nearby or just mentioned: *Take these toys to your room.* —*pronoun, plural* **these** A thing or person nearby or just mentioned: *This is our secret clubhouse.*

Thurs•day (thûrz′ dē) *or* (thûrz′ dā′) *noun, plural* **Thursdays** The fifth day of the week: *Art class meets every Thursday after school.*

time (tīm) *noun, plural* **times** **1.** All the days that have been and will ever be; the past, present, and future. **2.** A period in which something happens or continues. *Idiom.* **at times.** Now and then; once in a while: *At times I wish I lived in a different country.*

times (tīmz) *preposition* Multiplied by: *Three times two equals six.*

ti•ny (tī′ nē) *adjective* **tinier, tiniest** Very small: *The kitten was so tiny that it fit in my hand.*

tire¹ (tīr) *verb* **tired, tiring** To become weary: *Lee tired after hiking all day.*

tire² (tīr) *noun, plural* **tires** A band of rubber around the rim of a wheel: *My bicycle has a flat tire.*

Pronunciation Key

ă	pat	îr	deer	*th*	this
ā	pay	ŏ	pot	ŭ	cut
âr	care	ō	toe	ûr	urge
ä	father	ô	paw, for	ə	about,
ĕ	pet	oi	noise		item,
ē	bee	ŏŏ	took		edible,
ĭ	pit	ōō	boot		gallop,
ī	pie	ou	out		circus
		th	thin		

toast (tōst) *verb* **toasted, toasting** To brown by heating: *We toasted marshmallows over the campfire.* —*noun* A slice of bread heated and browned on both sides: *I always have toast with my cereal.*

toe (tō) *noun, plural* **toes** One of the five separate divisions of the foot: *Ellen put her big toe into the bath water to see if it was too hot.*

too (tōō) *adverb* **1.** Also; besides: *Adam had to make the salad and set the table, too.* **2.** Very: *This soup is too hot.* • **Too** sounds like **two.**

took Look up **take.**

tooth (tōōth) *noun, plural* **teeth** Any of the hard, white, bony parts in the mouth used for biting and chewing: *Brittany's front tooth is ready to fall out.*

tow•er (tou′ ər) *noun, plural* **towers** A high structure or a part of a building rising higher than the rest of it: *Rapunzel was hidden away in a tower so that no one could reach her.*

town (toun) *noun, plural* **towns** A group of houses or buildings that is larger than a village but smaller than a city: *My aunt is the new mayor of our town.*

toy (toi) *noun, plural* **toys** Something a child plays with: *Johnny's favorite toy is Robbie the Robot.*

train (trān) *noun, plural* **trains** Connected railroad cars pulled by an engine or powered by electricity: *The train left at 1:00 P.M.*

true (trōō) *adjective* **truer, truest** Not false; according to fact: *Only Marcel knows the true story.*

try (trī) *verb* **tries, tried, trying** To make an effort; to attempt: *Try to be brave.*

Tues·day (tōōz′ dē) *or* (tōōz′ dā′) *or* (tyōōz′ dē) *or* (tyōōz′ dā′) *noun, plural* **Tuesdays** The third day of the week: *I go to the library every Tuesday.*

turn (tûrn) *verb* **turned, turning**
1. To move round; rotate: *The earth turns on its axis once every 24 hours.* **2.** To change direction or position: *The path turned into the woods.* —*noun, plural* **turns** A chance to do something after someone else.

two (tōō) *noun* One more than one: *The twins are two of my good buddies.* • **Two** sounds like **too.**

un·der (ŭn′ dər) *preposition* **1.** Below; beneath: *I put my shoes under my bed.* **2.** Less than: *Sue was under 12 years old.*

use (yōōz) *verb* **used, using** To put into service: *I used all the toothpaste.*
    Idiom. **used to.** Familiar with: *I was used to sleeping with the light on.*

used (yōōzd) *adjective* Not new: *Nick bought a used bike.*

va·ri·e·ty (və rī′ ĭ tē) *noun, plural* **varieties 1.** A different kind within the same group: *We had a new variety of soup for lunch.* **2.** Change or difference: *I like variety in my day.*

ver·y (věr′ ē) *adverb* Much; extremely: *That joke was very funny.*

voice (vois) *noun, plural* **voices** The sound coming from the mouth: *Bernice has a wonderful voice.*

waf·fle (wŏf′ əl) *noun, plural* **waffles** A crisp cake made of batter: *Dad made waffles for breakfast.*

wait (wāt) *verb* **waited, waiting** To stay until someone comes or something happens: *We could hardly wait for the cartoon to start.* • **Wait** sounds like **weight.**

walk (wôk) *verb* **walked, walking** To go on foot at a steady pace: *The elephant walked slowly around the big circus tent.*

was (wŏz) *or* (wŭz) *or* (wəz) Look up **be.**

wash (wŏsh) *or* (wôsh) *verb* **washed, washing** To clean with water and sometimes soap: *I'll wash if you dry.*

was·n't (wŏz′ ənt) *or* (wŭz′ ənt) The contraction of "was not": *Bill wasn't ready when his friends arrived.*

wa·ter (wô′ tər) *or* (wŏt′ ər) *noun* **1.** The colorless, tasteless, odorless liquid that fills oceans, rivers, and ponds: *Water falls from the sky as rain.* **2.** A lake, river, pool, or any other body of this liquid: *We went for a swim in the water.* —*verb* **watered, watering** To sprinkle or provide with water: *The rain watered the grass for me.*

we'd (wēd) The contraction of "we had," "we should," or "we would": *We'd better call our parents before we walk home.*

Wednes·day (wěnz′ dē) *or* (wěnz′ dā′) *noun, plural* **Wednesdays** The fourth day of the week: *We will leave on Wednesday.*

weigh (wā) *verb* **weighed, weighing**
1. To find out how heavy something is by using a scale: *Mom lets me weigh all the vegetables before she buys them.* **2.** To have a certain weight: *Jason's dog weighs only 11 pounds.*

weird (wîrd) *adjective* **weirder, weirdest**
1. Causing an uneasy feeling; mysterious: *The noise from the cave was weirder today than yesterday.* **2.** Strange; odd; unusual: *That is the weirdest story I have ever read.*

we'll (wēl) The contraction of "we will" or "we shall": *We'll go into the fun house with you.*

well (wĕl) *adverb* **better, best** In a way that is good or correct: *I play the piano well. Diego plays better than I do. Simon plays best of all.*

were (wûr) Look up **be.**

were•n't (wûrnt) *or* (wûr′ ənt) The contraction of "were not": *My friends weren't home when I stopped by.*

we've (wĕv) The contraction of "we have": *We've still got a lot of work to do on the tree house.*

wharf (wôrf) *noun, plural* **wharves** A landing place for boats and ships built along a shore; dock: *Five boats were at the wharf.*

what (wŏt) *or* (wŭt) *or* (wət) *pronoun*
1. Which thing or things: *What do you want me to do?* **2.** The thing which: *I didn't know what she wanted.* **3.** Which: *What color do you want to paint your room?*

wheel (wēl) *noun, plural* **wheels**
A round frame supported by spokes on which a vehicle moves: *Have you ever been on the Ferris wheel?*

when (wĕn) *adverb* At what time: *When will you be ready to go?* —*conjunction* At a particular time: *Blink when I say your name.*

where (wâr) *adverb* **1.** At what place: *Where are my mittens?* **2.** To what place: *Where are we going on our class trip?*

where'd (wârd) The contraction of "where did": *Where'd you leave your coat?*

which (wĭch) *pronoun* **1.** What one or ones: *Which is mine?* **2.** The one or ones mentioned: *I bought my mom a gift, which I know she will like.* —*adjective* What one or ones: *Pam couldn't tell which hat was hers.*

while (wīl) *noun* A period of time: *Please stay for a while.* —*conjunction* **1.** At the same time that: *Mom read the newspaper while I did my homework.* **2.** Although: *Ron was short while his brothers were tall.*

white (wīt) *noun* The lightest color; the color of snow: *White is the color of clouds.* —*adjective* **whiter, whitest** Having the color white: *I have white shoes.*

who (hōō) *pronoun* What person or persons: *Who is your best friend?*

whole (hōl) *adjective* **1.** Not broken; complete: *Is this a whole deck of cards?* **2.** Entire amount: *I ate the whole pie by myself.* • **Whole** sounds like **hole.**

who'll (hōōl) The contraction of "who will" or "who shall": *Who'll bring the games?*

why (wī) *adverb* For what reason: *Why is your tongue green?*

width (wĭdth) *or* (wĭth) *or* (wĭtth) *noun, plural* **widths** The distance from side to side: *The width of the room is ten feet.*

wild•flow•er (wīld′ flou′ ər) *noun, plural* **wildflowers** Flowers on a wild plant: *The wildflowers were pretty.*

will (wĭl) *helping verb* **would** (wŏŏd)
To intend to; to mean to: *I will go to the picnic. I knew you would come sooner or later.*
• **Would** sounds like **wood.**

win (wĭn) *verb* **won** (wŭn), **winning**
To gain a victory: *Who won the art contest?*

win•ter (wĭn′ tər) *noun, plural* **winters**
The coldest season of the year, coming between fall and spring: *I don't like to shovel snow in the winter.*

wire (wīr) *noun, plural* **wires** Metal drawn out into a thin thread: *The fence around the farm was made of wire.*

wish (wĭsh) *noun, plural* **wishes** A strong desire: *Renee's only wish was to be finished with her work.* —*verb* **wished, wishing** To have a desire for something: *Ken wished he could meet his favorite singing star.*

won Look up **win.**

won't (wōnt) The contraction of "will not": *I won't be at the park today.*

wood (wŏŏd) *noun* The hard material making up the trunk and branches of a tree: *The cabin was built of wood.*
• **Wood** sounds like **would.**

word (wûrd) *noun, plural* **words** A sound or group of sounds having a certain meaning: *I missed only one word on my spelling test.*

work (wûrk) *noun* **1.** The effort made in doing or making something: *Mowing the lawn is hard work.* **2.** A task: *I can't go because I have too much school work to do.* —*verb* **worked, working** To have a job: *Joe worked at the supermarket every day after school.*

world (wûrld) *noun* The earth: *In history class we learn about the world.*

worm (wûrm) *noun, plural* **worms** A crawling creature with a long, slender body: *There are lots of worms in the backyard.*

would Look up **will.**

would•n't (wŏŏd′ nt) The contraction of "would not": *Simone knew she wouldn't get home on time unless she ran.*

would•'ve (wŏŏd′ əv) The contraction of "would have": *Jerrell would've cleaned his room, but he was late for school.*

write (rīt) *verb* **wrote** (rōt), **written, writing** To make letters or words with a pen, pencil, etc.: *Karen promised to write to*

me when she went on vacation. I wrote my name on my paper. • **Write** sounds like **right.**

wrote Look up **write.**

yard^1 (yärd) *noun, plural* **yards** A unit of length measuring 3 feet or 36 inches: *This room is 3 yards long.*

yard^2 (yärd) *noun, plural* **yards** A piece of land near a building: *My house has a big yard to play in.*

year (yîr) *noun, plural* **years** The length of time it takes the earth to go around the sun once; 365 days: *This year I will be 10 years old.*

yel•low (yĕl′ ō) *noun* The color of gold or butter: *Yellow is the color of ripe lemons.* —*adjective* **yellower, yellowest** Having this color: *I wore my yellow shirt with my blue pants.*

you'd (yŏŏd) The contraction of "you had" or "you would": *You'd better go to bed before you fall asleep in the chair.*

you'll (yŏŏl) *or* (yŏŏl) *or* (yəl) The contraction of "you will" or "you shall": *You broke this vase, so you'll have to pay for it.*

you've (yŏŏv) The contraction of "you have": *You've got a turtle just like mine.*